Practical Process Validation

Also available from ASQ Quality Press:

Handbook of Investigation and Effective CAPA Systems, Second Edition
José Rodríguez-Pérez

Implementing ISO/IEC 17025:2005: A Practical Guide
Bhavan "Bob" Mehta

Statistical Process Control for the FDA-Regulated Industry
Manuel E. Peña-Rodríguez

Practical Design of Experiments (DOE): A Guide for Optimizing Designs and Processes
Mark Allen Durivage

Quality Risk Management in the FDA-Regulated Industry
José Rodríguez-Pérez

Practical Attribute and Variable Measurement Systems Analysis (MSA): A Guide for Conducting Gage R&R Studies and Test Method Validations
Mark Allen Durivage

Practical Engineering, Process, and Reliability Statistics
Mark Allen Durivage

The Certified Pharmaceutical GMP Professional Handbook, Second Edition
FDC Division and Mark Allen Durivage, editor

The FDA and Worldwide Current Good Manufacturing Practices and Quality System Requirements Guidebook for Finished Pharmaceuticals
José Rodríguez-Pérez

Mastering and Managing the FDA Maze, Second Edition: Medical Device Overview
Gordon Harnack

Failure Mode and Effect Analysis: FMEA from Theory to Execution, Second Edition
D. H. Stamatis

Development of FDA-Regulated Medical Products, Second Edition: A Translational Approach
Elaine Whitmore

To request a complimentary catalog of ASQ Quality Press publications, call 800-248-1946, or visit our website at http://www.asq.org/quality-press.

Practical Process Validation

Mark A. Durivage
Bob (Bhavan) Mehta

ASQ Quality Press
Milwaukee, Wisconsin

American Society for Quality, Quality Press, Milwaukee 53203
© 2016 by ASQ
All rights reserved. Published 2016
Printed in the United States of America
22 21 20 19 18 17 16   5 4 3 2 1

Library of Congress Cataloging-in-Publication Data

Names: Durivage, Mark Allen, author. | Mehta, Bob, 1961– author.
Title: Practical process validation / Mark A. Durivage, Bob (Bhavan) Mehta.
Description: Milwaukee, Wisconsin : ASQ Quality Press, [2016] | Includes
  bibliographical references and index.
Identifiers: LCCN 2016022011 | ISBN 9780873899369 (hard cover : alk. paper)
Subjects: LCSH: Process control. | Production control. | Quality control.
Classification: LCC TS158.6 .D87 2016 | DDC 658.5—dc23
LC record available at https://lccn.loc.gov/2016022011

ISBN: 978-0-87389-936-9

No part of this book may be reproduced in any form or by any means, electronic, mechanical, photocopying, recording, or otherwise, without the prior written permission of the publisher.

Publisher: Seiche Sanders
Acquisitions Editor: Matt T. Meinholz
Managing Editor: Paul Daniel O'Mara
Production Administrator: Randall Benson

ASQ Mission: The American Society for Quality advances individual, organizational, and community excellence worldwide through learning, quality improvement, and knowledge exchange.

Attention Bookstores, Wholesalers, Schools, and Corporations: ASQ Quality Press books, video, audio, and software are available at quantity discounts with bulk purchases for business, educational, or instructional use. For information, please contact ASQ Quality Press at 800-248-1946, or write to ASQ Quality Press, P.O. Box 3005, Milwaukee, WI 53201-3005.

To place orders or to request ASQ membership information, call 800-248-1946. Visit our website at http://www.asq.org/quality-press.

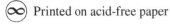 Printed on acid-free paper

Quality Press
600 N. Plankinton Ave.
Milwaukee, WI 53203-2914
E-mail: authors@asq.org
The Global Voice of Quality®

We would like to dedicate this book to all quality, engineering, manufacturing, and GMP compliance auditing professionals and professors/instructors teaching biomedical engineering courses around the world, and to the members of the American Society for Quality (ASQ).

Table of Contents

List of Figures and Tables xv
Preface xvii
Acknowledgments xix

Chapter 1 Introduction 1

Chapter 2 Regulatory and Certification Requirements 3
   2.1 FDA Requirements 4
      Subpart G—Production and Process Controls (Code of Federal
      Regulation 2014) 4
   2.2 Failing to Comply with FDA Requirements 7
      Examples of FDA Warning Letters with Form 483 Observations
      for §820.75 8
   2.3 ISO Requirements 10
      ISO 13485:2003 and EN ISO 13485:2012 10
   2.4 Path to Certification and Compliance 11
   2.5 Regulatory and Certification Requirements Summary 11

Chapter 3 Establishing Policies and Procedures 13
   3.1 The Purpose behind Establishing Process Validation Policies and
      Procedures 13
   3.2 Validation Policy Statements 14
   3.3 Recommended Procedures in Support of Practical Process
      Validation 15
   3.4 Writing the Process Validation Procedure 16
      Purpose 16
      Scope 17
      Definitions (Relevant to the Validation Process) 17
      References (Internal and External) 17
      Responsibilities 17
      Validation Requirements (Validation, Documentation) 18
      Process Flow (Validation Planning, Validation Process, IQ, OQ,
      PQ, and PPQ) 18
      Sample Size Rationale 19
      Data Collection, Statistical Methodology, and Analysis 19

Handling Deviations	19
Validation Report	20
Process Monitoring	20
Revalidation Requirements	20
3.5 Summary	21

Chapter 4 Validation Prerequisites **23**
- 4.1 Design of Experiments 23
- 4.2 Understanding the Importance of Calibration/Metrology 25
- 4.3 Ensuring That Test Method Validation (TMV) Activities Have Been Completed 27
- 4.4 Training 29
  - Basic Training Program Requirements 30
  - New Employee Orientation 30
  - Quality Management System Training 31
  - Career Development Training 31
  - Training Methodology 31
  - Documentation of Training 32
- 4.5 Third-Party Service Providers 32
- 4.6 Summary 32

Chapter 5 Process Validation Considerations **35**
- 5.1 Validation or Verification 35
  - 21 CFR, Part 820, Section 820.75—Process Validation 35
- 5.2 Process Validation Planning 36
- 5.3 Process Scoping 36
- 5.4 Installation Qualification 37
- 5.5 Operational Qualification 38
  - Equipment 38
  - Process 38
- 5.6 Performance Qualification 39
- 5.7 Process Performance Qualification 39
- 5.8 Statistical Methods for Data Collection and Analysis 40
- 5.9 Process Validation Reporting 40
- 5.10 Process Monitoring 40
- 5.11 Decision to Repeat Process Validation 40
- 5.12 Conclusion 41

Chapter 6 Validation Master Plan **43**
- 6.1 Validation Master Plan Content 43
- 6.2 Determining the Need for Validation 45
- 6.3 Conclusion 47

Chapter 7 Software Validation **49**
- 7.1 FDA Requirements for Software Validation 49
  - 21 CFR, Section 820.30—Design Controls 49

    21 CFR, Section 820.70—Production and Process Controls 50
    21 CFR, Part 11—Electronic Records; Electronic Signatures 50
  7.2 Determining the Need for Software Validation 50
  7.3 Software Development Life Cycle 52
    Requirements Phase 52
    Design and Development Phase 53
    Software Construction Phase 53
    Software Testing Phase 53
    Software Release Phase 53
    Final Review of the Traceability Matrix 53
  7.4 Creation of the User Requirements Document 54
  7.5 Development of the Project Plan—Master Validation Plan (MVP) 54
  7.6 Creation of the Functional Specifications Document 56
  7.7 Performance of the Gap Analysis 56
  7.8 Writing of the Installation Protocol 56
  7.9 Writing of the Installation Report 56
  7.10 Writing of the Testing Protocol(s)—Validation Protocols 57
  7.11 Final Test Report 57
  7.12 System Release/Go-Live 57
  7.13 Validation Completion 58
  7.14 Repeating Validation 58
  7.15 Summary 58

Chapter 8 Revalidation and Retrospective Validation **59**
  8.1 Retrospective Validation 61
  8.2 Revalidation 62
  8.3 Conclusion 63

Chapter 9 Sample Size Considerations **65**
  9.1 Sampling Plan Standards 66
  9.2 Sample Size Calculation Based on Confidence and Reliability with
    Zero Failures Allowed 66
  9.3 Reliability Estimate When Sample Size Is Provided 67
  9.4 Sample Size Calculation with Failures Allowed 67
  9.5 Reliability Estimate When Sample Sizes Are Specified 68
  9.6 Determining the Appropriate Number of Lots 69
  9.7 Conclusion 69

Chapter 10 Control Charts for Continuous Process Monitoring **71**
  10.1 Control Chart Types and Selection 71
  10.2 Control Chart Interpretation 71
  10.3 $\bar{X}$ and R Control Charts 73
  10.4 $\bar{X}$ and s Control Charts 78
  10.5 c-Charts 81
  10.6 u-Charts 83

10.7 *np*-Charts	86
10.8 *p*-Charts	88
10.9 *X* and mR (Moving Range) Control Charts	91
10.10 Conclusion	93

Chapter 11 Outliers 95
11.1 Outlier Detection Based on the Interquartile Range	95
11.2 Dixon's Q Test	96
11.3 Dean and Dixon Outlier Test	97
11.4 Grubbs Outlier Test	98
11.5 Walsh's Outlier Test	99
11.6 Hampel's Method for Outlier Detection	100
11.7 Conclusion	102

Chapter 12 Process Capability 103
12.1 Process Capability for Variables Data	103
12.2 Process Capability for Attributes Data	104
12.3 Conclusion	105

Chapter 13 Common Validation Issues 107
13.1 Line Clearance Not Performed	107
13.2 Deviations—Opening, Investigation, and Closing	107
13.3 Disposition of OQ Product Produced	108
13.4 Using a Simulant or Dunnage for OQ	108
13.5 Bracketing Strategy/Rationale for Family of Parts	108
13.6 First Article Layout (FAL)/First Article Inspection (FAI)	108
13.7 Not Producing Enough Samples	109
13.8 Not Recording the Lot Numbers of the Materials Used During the Validation	109
13.9 Training	109
13.10 Establishing Revalidation/Retrospective Validation Criteria and Intervals	109
13.11 Using Uncalibrated Inspection, Measuring, and Test Equipment (IMTE)	110
13.12 Not Verifying the Measurement System	110
13.13 Not Validating Identical Machines	110
13.14 Not Validating Identical Tooling	110
13.15 Approvals	111
13.16 Change Control	111
13.17 Not Planning/Performing Continuous Process Monitoring	111
13.18 Not Having a Validation Master Plan	111
13.19 Sample Size Not Justified	111
13.20 The Lack of Predefined Acceptance Criteria	112
13.21 Conclusion	112

Appendix A	**Distribution of the Chi-Square**	**113**
Appendix B	**Control Chart Constants**	**115**
Appendix C	**Critical Values of the Dean and Dixon Outlier Test**	**117**
Appendix D	**Critical Values for the Grubbs Outlier Test**	**119**

Glossary *121*
Bibliography *133*
Index *137*

List of Figures and Tables

Figure 1.1	Medical device process validation FDA form 483 ranking 2006–2014.	1
Figure 3.1	Example of a process validation policy statement for the quality policy manual.	15
Figure 3.2	Example of a training policy statement for the quality policy manual.	15
Figure 3.3	Process validation decision tree.	18
Figure 3.4	Process validation purpose statements.	19
Figure 4.1	Cause-and-effect diagram depicting inputs (X's) and outputs (Y's).	25
Table 4.1	Hypothesis truth table.	25
Figure 4.2	Possible sources of process variation.	27
Figure 6.1	Validation documentation hierarchy.	43
Table 6.1	Example master validation list.	45
Figure 6.2	Process validation decision tree.	46
Figure 7.1	Software development life cycle phases.	52
Figure 7.2	Software validation decision tree—legacy software.	55
Figure 7.3	Software validation decision tree—new software.	55
Figure 8.1	Typical process validation life cycle.	59
Figure 9.1	Comparison of variable and attribute sample sizes with equivalent protection.	65
Table 10.1	Variables and attributes control charts selection.	72
Figure 10.1	Stable and unstable processes.	72
Figure 10.2	Control chart interpretation rules.	74
Figure 10.3	Control chart accuracy and precision.	75
Figure 10.4	Accuracy versus precision.	75
Table 10.2	Data for $\bar{X}$ and R chart.	76
Figure 10.5	$\bar{X}$ and R chart example.	77
Table 10.3	Data for $\bar{X}$ and s chart.	79
Figure 10.6	$\bar{X}$ and s chart example.	80
Table 10.4	Data for c-chart.	82
Figure 10.7	c-chart example.	83

Table 10.5	Data for u-chart.	84
Figure 10.8	u-chart example.	85
Table 10.6	Data for np-chart.	87
Figure 10.9	np-chart example.	88
Table 10.7	Data for p-chart.	89
Figure 10.10	p-chart example.	90
Table 10.8	Data for $\bar{X}$ and mR chart.	92
Figure 10.11	$\bar{X}$ and mR chart example.	93
Table 11.1	Selected critical Q values.	97
Figure 12.1	Capable process versus not capable process.	103
Figure 12.2	Relationship between statistical control limits and product specifications.	104
Figure 12.3	Graphical relationship of process capability ratios.	105

Preface

The intent of this book is to provide manufacturing quality professionals working in virtually any industry a quick, convenient, and comprehensive guide to properly conducting process validations. Although not the primary focus of this book, software validation requirements are briefly discussed. The reader must keep in mind that validating software can be extremely challenging and that some of the tools and techniques presented for process validation may not be applicable to software validation.

Additionally, this book is intended to provide both background on and the requirements necessary to performing process validations that will comply with regulatory and certification body requirements. It is the authors' contention that decision making on and evaluation of process validations should be done in the context of a systems approach.

Acknowledgments

Mark A. Durivage—I would like to thank those who have inspired, taught, and trained me throughout my academic and professional career. Additionally, I would like to thank ASQ Quality Press, especially Matt Meinholz, Acquisitions Editor, and Paul Daniel O'Mara, Managing Editor, for their expertise and technical competence, which made this project a reality. I also wish to recognize my friend, colleague, author of *Implementing ISO/IEC 17025:2005*, and fellow ASQ Fellow Bhavan "Bob" Mehta, Principal Consultant at GMP ISO Expert Services, for coauthoring this book. Lastly, I would like to acknowledge the patience of my wife Dawn and my sons Jack and Sam, which allowed me the time to research and cowrite *Practical Process Validation*.

Bob Mehta—I was inspired to author this book when providing services as a consultant to my pharmaceutical, biotechnology, medical device, active pharmaceutical ingredient, dietary supplement, and food clients. I would like to thank my wife Nina and my son Jay for their love and support for the past several decades, including my time authoring this book. I would like to recognize my friend and colleague Mark Durivage, author of several books and ASQ Fellow, for coauthoring this book. I would also like to recognize faculty members of the MS in quality assurance program at Cal State Dominguez Hills and Cal Poly Pomona where I teach as an adjunct professor.

The authors would also like to thank Diane Goiffon, Software Quality Engineer, Melvin Alexander, Analytician, and Scott Glait, Senior Quality Assurance Engineer, for their reviews, which provided valuable insight on this book.

LIMIT OF LIABILITY/DISCLAIMER OF WARRANTY

The authors have put forth their best efforts in compiling the content of this book; however, no warranty with respect to the material's accuracy or completeness is made. Additionally, no warranty is made in regard to applying the recommendations made in this book to any business structure or environments. Businesses should consult regulatory, quality, and/or legal professionals prior to deciding on the appropriateness of advice and recommendations made within this book. The authors shall not be held liable for loss of profit or other commercial damages resulting from the employment of recommendations made within this book, including special, incidental, consequential, or other damages.

1
Introduction

This book was written to assist quality technicians, engineers, managers, and others that need to plan, conduct, and monitor validation activities. To that end, the intent of this book is to provide the quality professional working in virtually any industry a quick, convenient, and comprehensive guide to properly conducting process validations that meet regulatory and certification requirements. Both authors currently work in the medical device industry; however, the concepts presented in this book are designed for a broader audience.

This book provides an introduction and background to the requirements necessary to perform process validations that will comply with regulatory and certification body requirements. It is the authors' contention that decision making on and evaluation of process validations should be done in the context of a *systems* approach.

From 2006–2015, process validation issues ranked within the top six of FDA form 483 observation findings (see Figure 1.1) issued by the Food and Drug Administration (FDA) each year. This poses a substantial problem for the medical device industry and is the reason the authors wanted to write this book and share their collective knowledge: to help organizations improve patient safety and increase profitability while maintaining a state of compliance with regulations and standards.

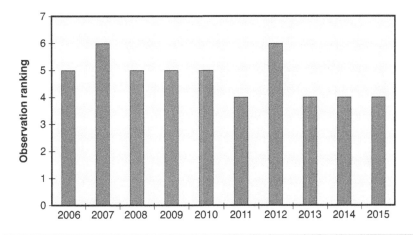

Figure 1.1 Medical device process validation FDA form 483 ranking 2006–2015.
Source: Compiled from http://www.fda.gov/ICECI/Inspections/ucm250720.htm.

2
Regulatory and Certification Requirements

Quality and manufacturing engineers already understand the value of process validation and the need to ensure that product features, which cannot be fully verified through inspection or test, need to be validated. Additionally, the validation process must be robust and, of course, well documented. Although not a topic for discussion in this book, the validation process really commences during the design and development of product. For example, establishments tasked with the design and development of finished medical devices are required to employ design verification and design validation activities as part of the overall design and development methodology. In fact, the transfer of finished medical devices to commercialization cannot occur until all design and development activities have been successfully completed. The expectation of manufacturing personnel is that the product design being transferred has been designed and developed with all applicable features being appropriately verified and validated; otherwise, the product is not ready for transfer.

Furthermore, there are regulatory and statutory considerations associated with the validation of finished medical devices. Within the United States, device establishments are expected to comply with FDA's Quality System Regulation (QSR) requirements. In accordance with 21 CFR, Part 820, Section 820.75 (Process Validation), the regulation clearly states: *"where the results of a process cannot be fully verified by subsequent inspection and test, the process shall be validated with a high degree of assurance"* (Code of Federal Regulation 2014). Part 11 (Electronic Records; Electronic Signatures) requirements must also be considered when working with computer-generated records and the validation of computer systems and software that produce electronic records.

Similar requirements exist in regulatory and statutory requirements employed by regulatory bodies outside of the United States, for example: (a) Japan's MHLW Ministerial Ordinance 169, Article 45; (b) Health Canada's SOR/98-282 standard's direct reference to complying with ISO 13485:2003; and (c) Brazil's RDC 16/2013 (*Technical Regulation for Good Manufacturing Practices of Medical Devices and In Vitro Diagnostic Devices*). Each references the requirement for process validation activities to be performed.

Finally, the European notified bodies recognize the requirements for certification of ISO 13485. Compliance with these standards, depending on a device establishment's location, is a requirement for entering medical devices into commerce in the European Union. Similarly to the FDA's process validation requirements delineated within the QSR, *Validation of Processes for Production and Service Provision* of ISO 9001 and

ISO 13485 details specific requirements for process validation, including computer software, record retention requirements, and environmental controls.

2.1 FDA REQUIREMENTS

It would be a daunting task to separate Section 820.75 from the rest of the regulatory requirements detailed under Subpart G of Part 820, Quality System Regulation, so as the authors, we decided it was best for clarification purposes to include the entire subpart in support of a providing a better understanding of the FDA's process validation requirements. In fact, understanding the requirements for production and process controls, including inspection, measuring, and test equipment requirements is critical because each become inputs into the process validation protocols. Please keep in mind that production and process changes, personnel, contamination control, buildings, equipment, manufacturing materials, automated process, and the calibration of inspection, measuring, and test equipment are contributing factors to process validation.

Subpart G—Production and Process Controls (Code of Federal Regulation 2014)

Section 820.70 Production and Process Controls

(a) *General.* Each manufacturer shall develop, conduct, control, and monitor production processes to ensure that a device conforms to its specifications. Where deviations from device specifications could occur as a result of the manufacturing process, the manufacturer shall establish and maintain process control procedures that describe any process controls necessary to ensure conformance to specifications. Where process controls are needed they shall include:

(1) Documented instructions, standard operating procedures (SOPs), and methods that define and control the manner of production;

(2) Monitoring and control of process parameters and component and device characteristics during production;

(3) Compliance with specified reference standards or codes;

(4) The approval of processes and process equipment; and

(5) Criteria for workmanship which shall be expressed in documented standards or by means of identified and approved representative samples.

(b) *Production and process changes.* Each manufacturer shall establish and maintain procedures for changes to a specification, method, process, or procedure. Such changes shall be verified or where appropriate validated according to 820.75, before implementation and these activities shall be documented. Changes shall be approved in accordance with 820.40.

(c) *Environmental control.* Where environmental conditions could reasonably be expected to have an adverse effect on product quality, the manufacturer shall establish and maintain procedures to adequately control these environmental conditions. Environmental control system(s) shall be periodically inspected to verify that the system, including necessary equipment, is adequate and functioning properly. These activities shall be documented and reviewed.

d) *Personnel.* Each manufacturer shall establish and maintain requirements for the health, cleanliness, personal practices, and clothing of personnel if contact between such personnel and product or environment could reasonably be expected to have an adverse effect on product quality. The manufacturer shall ensure that maintenance and other personnel who are required to work temporarily under special environmental conditions are appropriately trained or supervised by a trained individual.

(e) *Contamination control.* Each manufacturer shall establish and maintain procedures to prevent contamination of equipment or product by substances that could reasonably be expected to have an adverse effect on product quality.

(f) *Buildings.* Buildings shall be of suitable design and contain sufficient space to perform necessary operations, prevent mix-ups, and assure orderly handling.

(g) *Equipment.* Each manufacturer shall ensure that all equipment used in the manufacturing process meets specified requirements and is appropriately designed, constructed, placed, and installed to facilitate maintenance, adjustment, cleaning, and use.

(1) *Maintenance schedule.* Each manufacturer shall establish and maintain schedules for the adjustment, cleaning, and other maintenance of equipment to ensure that manufacturing specifications are met. Maintenance activities, including the date and individual(s) performing the maintenance activities, shall be documented.

(2) *Inspection.* Each manufacturer shall conduct periodic inspections in accordance with established procedures to ensure adherence to applicable equipment maintenance schedules. The inspections, including the date and individual(s) conducting the inspections, shall be documented.

(3) *Adjustment.* Each manufacturer shall ensure that any inherent limitations or allowable tolerances are visibly posted on or near equipment requiring periodic adjustments or are readily available to personnel performing these adjustments.

(h) *Manufacturing material.* Where a manufacturing material could reasonably be expected to have an adverse effect on product quality, the manufacturer shall establish and maintain procedures for the use and removal of such manufacturing material to ensure that it is removed or limited to an amount that does not adversely affect the device's quality. The removal or reduction of such manufacturing material shall be documented.

(i) *Automated processes.* When computers or automated data processing systems are used as part of production or the quality system, the manufacturer shall validate computer software for its intended use according to an established protocol. All software changes shall be validated before approval and issuance. These validation activities and results shall be documented.

Section 820.72 Inspection, Measuring, and Test Equipment

(a) *Control of inspection, measuring, and test equipment.* Each manufacturer shall ensure that all inspection, measuring, and test equipment, including mechanical, automated, or electronic inspection and test equipment, is suitable for its intended purposes and is capable of producing valid results. Each manufacturer shall establish and maintain procedures to ensure that equipment is routinely calibrated, inspected, checked, and maintained. The procedures shall include provisions for handling, preservation, and storage of equipment, so that its accuracy and fitness for use are maintained. These activities shall be documented.

(b) *Calibration.* Calibration procedures shall include specific directions and limits for accuracy and precision. When accuracy and precision limits are not met, there shall be provisions for remedial action to reestablish the limits and to evaluate whether there was any adverse effect on the device's quality. These activities shall be documented.

(1) *Calibration standards.* Calibration standards used for inspection, measuring, and test equipment shall be traceable to national or international standards. If national or international standards are not practical or available, the manufacturer shall use an independent reproducible standard. If no applicable standard exists, the manufacturer shall establish and maintain an in-house standard.

(2) *Calibration records.* The equipment identification, calibration dates, the individual performing each calibration, and the next calibration date shall be documented. These records shall be displayed on or near each piece of equipment or shall be readily available to the personnel using such equipment and to the individuals responsible for calibrating the equipment.

Section 820.75 Process Validation

(a) Where the results of a process cannot be fully verified by subsequent inspection and test, the process shall be validated with a high degree of assurance and approved according to established procedures. The validation activities and results, including the date and signature of the individual(s) approving the validation and where appropriate the major equipment validated, shall be documented.

(b) Each manufacturer shall establish and maintain procedures for monitoring and control of process parameters for validated processes to ensure that the specified requirements continue to be met.

(1) Each manufacturer shall ensure that validated processes are performed by qualified individual(s).

(2) For validated processes, the monitoring and control methods and data, the date performed, and, where appropriate, the individual(s) performing the process or the major equipment used shall be documented.

(c) When changes or process deviations occur, the manufacturer shall review and evaluate the process and perform revalidation where appropriate. These activities shall be documented.

2.2 FAILING TO COMPLY WITH FDA REQUIREMENTS

For establishments that fail to comply with the QSR's requirements for process validation (§820.75), the penalties could be as benign as a form 483 observation or, depending on the overall inspection results, an agency Warning Letter. If an establishment receives a form 483 observation, it is vitally important that a well-written response is provided to the FDA within 15 days of receipt. If a Warning Letter is forthcoming, the same 15-day response time is required. When responding to FDA, device establishments should ensure that the response contains the following elements:

- A restatement or clear description of the problem
- Containment activities being pursued
- Root cause investigation
- Actions to be pursued to prevent recurrence
- Verification of effectiveness, and
- Documented evidence of correction activities pursued

In many cases, if the response(s) to the original form 483 observation is well written, it can actually reduce the chances of a Warning Letter being issued. However, if a Warning Letter is the end result of an inspection, be reminded that a Warning Letter is a tool provided by FDA to grab management's attention and to ensure that the establishment focuses on quality, regulatory, and statutory requirements in support of bringing the *quality management system* (QMS) into compliance.

It is imperative to understand the basis for the form 483 observation and thoroughly address the issue(s) raised in the response. However, also ensure that the actions/promises documented in the response can be accomplished within the timeline promised to the Agency. Do *not* overpromise and under-deliver. A best practice is to use a Gantt chart in the response. The chart will provide the Agency a visual timeline of commitments and promises made and an understanding of the steps the company feels necessary to resolve the issue(s).

Examples of FDA Warning Letters with Form 483 Observations for §820.75

Warning Letter Dated December 9, 2014

Observation One (1) "Failure to validate with a high degree of assurance, a process which results cannot be fully verified by subsequent inspection and test, as required by 21 CFR Part 820.75(a). According to your firm's documentation, the requalification of the Ethylene Oxide (EtO) Sterilization Cycle (b)(4) Protocol and Report (b)(4) and REV (b)(4), dated 05/10/2013 and 06/05/2013 respectively, was performed according to (b)(4) to qualify the terminal sterilization of the medical device/convenience kits. Per (b)(4), the sterilization of your convenience kits is deficient because Protocol and Report (b)(4) and (b)(4) does not demonstrate that critical factors were adequately considered. For example:

a. Your firm did not perform post-sterilization inspection as part of the performance requalification study to determine if the sterilization process adversely impacted product functionality and packaging integrity. According to the "Process Re-Qualification for Customed Soft Cycle," Final Report # (b)(4), dated 06/05/2013, "No physical inspection was conducted (b)(4) product."

b. SOP (b)(4), "Esterilización por Oxido de Etileno" (translation: EtO Sterilization), allows the load configuration to be sterilized to contain different convenience packs, combined (b)(4). The Process Re-Qualification for Customed Soft Cycle Validation documents (Protocol and Report (b)(4) and (b)(4), dated 05/10/2013 and 06/05/2013), state "The products selected represent a reference load selection for actual Customed product." There is no justification to support:

i. Product packages used during the Process Qualification (b)(4) sterilize product package configurations (b)(4);

ii. The load type and load configuration used during the Process Qualification represent (b)(4)

c. Your firm has provided installation and operational qualification protocols for (b)(4). The data provided appears to contain factual errors such as, (b)(4). Therefore, it's not possible to effectively determine whether the data provided is sufficient to support the (b)(4) qualification and sealing process validation.

We reviewed your firm's response dated August 21, 2014, and it's not adequate. While your firm initiated Corrective Action and Preventive Action (CAPA) (b)(4) to perform an EtO sterilization Soft Cycle (b)(4) and committed to generate a protocol that follows the new Revision of ISO 11135: (R) 2014, your firm's response is deficient, because it failed to address each of these issues and it's unclear whether the protocol was developed and fully implemented, and which requirements from ISO 11135 will be in the new requalification protocol. The corrective action does not describe the specific sterilization process that will be used to sterilize medical devices and kits after requalification of the EtO Sterilization Soft cycle. In addition, the corrective action does not describe how the sterilization cycles are validated and revalidated to ensure a Sterility Assurance Level (SAL) (b)(4). We reviewed your firm's response and conclude that it is not adequate. Your firm's response dated August 21, 2014, did not address item "c" (FDA Enforcement Page 2014)."

Warning Letter Dated December 8, 2014

Observation Four (4) "Failure to ensure that when the results of a process cannot be fully verified by subsequent inspection and test, the process shall be validated with a high degree of assurance and approved according to established procedure, as required by 21 CFR 820.75(a). For example:

a. Your firm performs a leak test, using an in-house test method, to verify the integrity of an (b)(4) in your OxySure canisters as part of your production monitoring activities. You stated you have not validated this test method.

b. Your firm uses (b)(4) processes to (b)(4) components/assemblies of your OxySure portable oxygen generator including the (b)(4). Your firm does not have evidence the (b)(4) processes used for these components have been validated.

c. Your firm uses a (b)(4) process to adhere various components of the OxySure portable oxygen generator to the cartridge, such as the (b)(4). Your firm does not have records showing you conducted a qualification of the (b)(4) Machine that is used for curing the (b)(4) or records showing you fully characterized the process to demonstrate it was capable of producing bonds that withstand the forces exerted during storage and use.

d. Your firm uses (b)(4) process to strengthen the (b)(4) that are part of your OxySure portable oxygen generator. Your firm did not have records showing you qualified the performance of your final established process parameters such as temperature and time.

We reviewed your firm's response and conclude that it is not adequate. Although you have committed to improving your validation of the (b)(4) and (b)(4) processes, you have not identified how you will correct your overall process validation practices moving forward to ensure process validations are conducted correctly in the future. Also, your response does not address how you will correct lack of validation for your test methods, such as the "Leak Test" identified on the FDA form 483. Further, you did not provide any evidence or commitments that you have conducted a full review of all your processes which are required to be validated to ensure they have been adequately validated (FDA Enforcement Page 2014).

2.3 ISO REQUIREMENTS

The ISO requirements enforced by notified bodies during a QMS audit are considerably more forgiving. Unlike FDA—which performs inspections, collects documented evidence of noncompliant issues that can be used in federal court, and issues form 483 observations and Warning Letters for compliance issues—notified bodies issue nonconformances (minor or major). Since the relationship between device establishments and notified bodies is defined by a written contract, coupled with the fact that device establishments pay their notified bodies for their audits, the relationship tends to be less contentious versus that with the FDA. However, compliance with ISO 13485 remains a requirement for establishments wishing to enter their products into commerce in the European Union and other regulatory markets recognizing the value of a notified body certification for ISO 13485, and the use of their notified body's Conformité Européenne (CE) Mark.

ISO 13485:2003 and EN ISO 13485:2012

7.5.2 Validation of Processes for Production and Service Provision (ISO 13485:2003)

7.5.2.1 General Requirements

The organization shall validate any processes for production and service provision where the resulting output cannot be verified by subsequent monitoring or measurement. This includes any processes where deficiencies become apparent only after the product is in use or the service has been delivered.

Validation shall demonstrate the ability of these processes to achieve planned results.

The organization shall establish arrangements for these processes including, as applicable:

a) Defined criteria for review and approval of the processes;

b) Approval of equipment and qualification of personnel;

c) Use of specific methods and procedures;

d) Requirements for records; and

e) Revalidation.

The organization shall establish documented procedures for the validation of the application of computer software (and changes to such software and/or its application) for production and service provision that affect the ability of the product to conform to specified requirements. Such software applications shall be validated prior to initial use.

Records of validation shall be maintained (reference 4.2.4 of ISO 13485).

2.4 PATH TO CERTIFICATION AND COMPLIANCE

The path toward certification and compliance is a relatively simple one. For starters, within the FDA the concept of *certification* does not exist; there is only *compliance*. If a device establishment enters Class II and Class III (and some Class I) products into commerce in the United States, then compliance with the QSR, which contains process validation requirements in accordance with §820.75, is a fundamental requirement. If a device establishment practices process validation in accordance with standards, regulations, and guidances, then compliance (although never guaranteed) should be achievable.

For ISO 13485, the notified body is tasked with issuing a certificate of conformity. For example, depending on classification, a device establishment will need a certificate reflecting their compliance with ISO 13485 and a separate accreditation for compliance with 93/42/EEC (the European Medical Device Directive), also known as the MDD. Similarly to FDA's approach to compliance, unless otherwise noted as a previously approved exclusion from the notified body, Clause 7.5.2 will be a requirement.

Regardless of a device establishment's compliance and certification needs, compliance with process validation requirements begins with establishing robust policies and procedures, the topic of the next chapter of this book. A successful approach to process validation begins with:

- Well-written policies and procedures
- Personnel that are appropriately trained to perform process validation
- Robust processes

Every aspect of process validation must be appropriately defined in established policies and procedures in order for establishments to be successful in their pursuit of creating robust processes that are capable of producing finished medical devices that are safe and effective in their intended use. Regulators will take the time to review the written protocols and test reports for:

- IQ—installation qualification
- OQ—operational qualification
- PQ—performance qualification
- PPQ—process performance qualification

2.5 REGULATORY AND CERTIFICATION REQUIREMENTS SUMMARY

Regardless of the regulatory pathway a device establishment has chosen to pursue, establishing a robust approach to process validation will be essential. In order to manufacture finished medical devices that are safe and effective in their intended use, device establishments need to perform some level of process validation, with a high degree of assurance, for each feature where the results of each process cannot be fully verified by subsequent inspection and test. In accordance with defined regulatory and statutory requirements, a device establishment's approach to process validation shall be documented in written policies and procedures. However, make no mistake, the FDA, a device establishment's notified body, and other regulators from around the globe will review a device establishment's approach to process validation and the resulting output of process validation, including the written protocols and tests reports for IQ, OQ, PQ, and PPQ. For device establishments that clearly understand the value of process validation (PV), the acronym PV will quickly become a manufacturing manager's favorite. Device establishments that fail to grasp the intrinsic value of PV will see some level of regulatory noncompliance in their future. It should also be noted that even if a process is validated, the manufacturer is still expected to monitor the process, that is, with in-process inspection and continuous process monitoring.

3

Establishing Policies and Procedures

The process of establishing policies and procedures begins with a fundamental understanding of the applicable regulatory and statutory requirements associated with process validation, including the applicable ISO standards. FDA has a very specific definition for the term *"establish."* In accordance with 21 CFR, Part 820, Section 820.3, *"establish means define, document (in writing or electronically), and implement"* (Code of Federal Regulation 2014). Additionally, the US FDA provides definitions for the terms (a) *"validation,"* which means confirmation by examination and provision of objective evidence that the particular requirements for a specific intended use can be consistently fulfilled, and (b) *"process validation,"* which means establishing by objective evidence that a process consistently produces a result or product meeting its predetermined specifications. When establishing the policies and procedures for process validation, it is imperative that the regulatory and statutory requirements become an integral component of the quality policy manual and high-level *standard operating procedures* (SOPs). However, where the proverbial rubber meets the road, the three essential requirements of effective process validation come into play:

- Initial process design
- Process qualification
- Ongoing process verification

3.1 THE PURPOSE BEHIND ESTABLISHING PROCESS VALIDATION POLICIES AND PROCEDURES

Keep in mind that the fundamental purpose of process validation is to ensure that process inputs support process outputs, resulting in a robust and repeatable process. Additionally, process validation is never a static process but rather a dynamic process that is subject to change premised on the data collected as part of the day-to-day manufacturing activities performed. According to recently released FDA process validation guidance for the pharma industry, process validation should be aligned with the agency's product life cycle concept (Guidance 2011). However, a thorough understanding of all of the following is required to successfully write effective policies and procedures:

- Design of experiments (DOE)
- Calibration/metrology
- Installation qualification (IQ)
- Operational qualification (OQ)
- Performance qualification (PQ)
- Process performance qualification (PPQ)
- Test method validation (TMV)

3.2 VALIDATION POLICY STATEMENTS

The policy statement is essentially going to be nothing more than the acknowledgment of the requirement in a high-level document, typically the quality policy manual for a medical device establishment. When drafting the policy statement, a simple but eloquent approach for writing a policy statement is a six-step approach. The steps required to write a robust policy statement consist of:

1. Identification of the requirement
2. Identifying the stakeholders needed to write the policy
3. Creating an outline of the essential points of the policy
4. Identifying the individual tasked with the actual writing of the policy statement
5. Scheduling a team meeting to review the rough draft
6. Incorporating and disseminating the policy to all members of the organization (Lorette 2015)

An example of a policy statement that aligns with the ISO 9001 and 13485 requirements is shown in Figure 3.1. The policy statement for process validation is typical of what most device establishments will incorporate into their quality policy manual.

Additionally, training is a requirement when pursuing process validation and verification activities. Regulators will often verify that device establishment personnel tasked with the writing of process validation and verification protocols and personnel tasked with the actual execution of process validation and approval of protocols are technically competent and appropriately trained. Documented evidence of training should also be captured in a policy statement placed into a device establishment's quality policy manual. Because training is such an important deliverable associated with process validation, it is recommended that the policy statement for training also contain a pointer specific to process validation and verification activities. An example of a robust training policy statement, which includes the recommended pointer to process validation and verification, can be found in Figure 3.2.

7.5.2 Validation of Processes for Production and Service Provision

Medical Device Establishment's Name shall validate any processes for production and service provision where the resulting output cannot be verified by subsequent inspection or test. This includes processes where deficiencies become apparent only after the finished medical device is employed in its intended use. Validation shall demonstrate the ability of these processes to achieve planned results.

Medical Device Establishment's Name shall establish procedures for the following elements associated with process validation:

- The criteria for the review and approval of processes
- Approval of equipment and qualification of personnel
- Use of specific methods and procedures
- Monitoring and control of parameters for validated processes, revalidation
- The requirements for records shall include the monitoring and control methods, the equipment used, and the date and signature(s) of the person(s) performing and approving the validation

Medical Device Establishment's Name shall establish documented procedures for the validation of sterilization processes. Sterilization processes shall be validated prior to their initial use.

Note: Records of sterilization validations shall be maintained.

Figure 3.1 Example of a process validation policy statement for the quality policy manual.

6.2.2. Competence, Awareness, and Training

Medical Device Establishment's Name shall document procedures for identifying training needs, and methods for ensuring that all personnel receive the appropriate level of training necessary for the successful execution of assigned responsibilities. The training provided by *Medical Device Establishment's Name* shall be effective. A training procedure shall document training requirements and procedures. *Medical Device Establishment's Name* personnel shall, as part of their training, be made aware of:

- Device defects that occur due to the improper performance of their specific jobs
- Errors and defects that may be encountered during the execution of validation and verification activities

Medical Device Establishment's Name personnel performing specific tasks (for example, process validation) where special skills or knowledge are needed, shall be qualified on the basis of education, training, and/or experience.

All records associated with training shall be maintained in accordance with *Medical Device Establishment's Name* record retention procedure.

Figure 3.2 Example of a training policy statement for the quality policy manual.

3.3 RECOMMENDED PROCEDURES IN SUPPORT OF PRACTICAL PROCESS VALIDATION

It is not sufficient to just have a process validation procedure as there are multiple influencers that will impact the pursuit of practical process validation. For example, *design of experiments* (DOE), calibration/metrology, and *test method validation* (TMV) will be important requirements necessary for the pursuit of process validation. Additionally, the actual process validation procedure needs to address the *four Q's* associated with practical process validation: IQ, OQ, PQ, and PPQ. DOE and TMV activities should have written standard operating procedures (SOPs) and/or work instructions (WIs).

3.4 WRITING THE PROCESS VALIDATION PROCEDURE

Before beginning work on writing the actual validation procedure, an outline for procedure content should be created. Note that 21 CFR, Part 820.72 does not specify specific sections; however, it is recommended that the following sections be considered for a process validation procedure:

- Purpose
- Scope
- Definitions (relevant to the validation process)
- References (internal and external)
- Responsibilities
- Validation Requirements (validation, documentation)
- Process Flow (validation planning, validation process, IQ, OQ, PQ, and PPQ)
- Sample Size Rationale
- Data Collection, Statistical Methodology, and Analysis
- Handling Deviations
- Validation Report
- Process Monitoring
- Revalidation Requirements

Purpose

Writing the procedure for process validation begins with the creation of a purpose statement. The purpose statement for an SOP should clearly state the purpose of the procedure. An example of a purpose statement for a process validation SOP is "This procedure delineates the validation of production equipment, utilities, and processes. It provides guidance for: (a) the development of validation master plans, (b) validation protocols, and (c) validation protocols."

Scope

Similarly to the purpose statement, the scope needs to be simple and to the point. In fact, the scope statement should not exceed one sentence. An example of a scope statement for a process validation procedure is "This procedure encompasses validation protocols (IQ, OQ, PQ, and PPQ), validation reports, and the revalidation of manufacturing equipment, utilities, and processes."

Definitions (Relevant to the Validation Process)

Best practice is for an organization to incorporate all definitions in a definitions procedure. However, some organizations prefer to place all relevant definitions into specific procedures. Regardless of the approach employed for the delineation of applicable definitions, and whether included in the process validation procedure or not, it is recommended that, as a minimum, the definitions employed by the US FDA in Section 820.3, "Definitions," of 21 CFR, Part 820 be included.

References (Internal and External)

References included in the process validation procedure should include internal and external documents. For example, internal procedures and/or work instructions, such as (a) risk management, (b) design controls, (c) control of measuring and monitoring equipment, (d) training, and (e) inspection and acceptance criteria, should be considered. For external references, regulations and standards to be considered include:

- 21 CFR Part 820, Quality System Regulation
- ISO 13485:2003 (2012 or 2016) *Medical devices—Quality management systems—Requirements for regulatory purposes*
- ISO 9001:2008 (2015) *Quality management system—Requirements*
- EN ISO 14971:2012 *Medical devices—Application of risk management to medical devices*

Responsibilities

The responsibilities should be defined premised on the use of generic but relevant statements. For example, *"Engineering"* is responsible for the review, revision, and execution of validation protocols, and adherence to validation activities delineated within this procedure. Another example would be *"Quality Assurance"* is responsible for the review and approval of validation protocols, deviations, and validation reports.

Validation Requirements (Validation, Documentation)

The validation requirements section of the procedure should contain the requirements for the handling of all documentation associated with each validation. For example, the documentation to be collected, the document retention process, and storage location should be captured. Additionally, the need for a master validation report (MVR) should be discussed.

Process Flow (Validation Planning, Validation Process, IQ, OQ, PQ, and PPQ)

A process flowchart known as a *decision tree* can be generated that results in a pictorial representation of the process validation process. Figure 3.3 depicts a simple flowchart that captures the need to perform process validation.

Process validation consists of four parts: the IQ, OQ, PQ, and PPQ. It is strongly recommended that a separate protocol be written for each validated process. As a minimum, the protocol should delineate the requirements for (a) the sample size (including rationale), (b) the equipment being used, (c) the risk index, (d) test methods employed, (e) predefined acceptance criteria, and (f) training requirements.

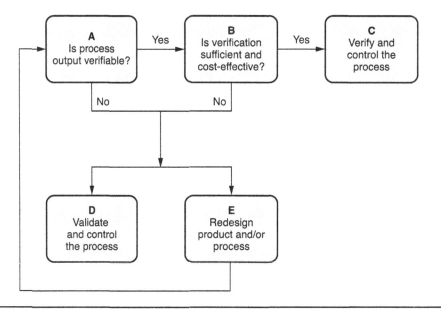

Figure 3.3 Process validation decision tree.
Source: Adapted from GHTF Study Group 3. 2004. *Quality Management Systems—Process Validation Guidance.* 2nd ed.

> 1.0 The purpose of *IQ* is to determine, through documented evidence, that all systems and equipment are installed correctly.
>
> 2.0 The purpose of *OQ* is to establish, by objective evidence, that the equipment process control limits meet all predetermined requirements. The operational qualification also challenges the process parameters (often referred to as "limits" or "worst-case" testing) to make sure they result in a product that meets all defined requirements under all anticipated conditions of manufacturing.
>
> 3.0 The purpose of *PQ* is to demonstrate that a process will consistently produce acceptable product under normal operating conditions. *Note: PQ testing must take place at nominal process conditions.*
>
> 4.0 The purpose of *PPQ* is to demonstrate that all validated processes produce end product that meets product specifications. PPQ looks at an entire manufacturing process versus a single process. Complete product configurations are built in accordance with nominal process conditions.

Figure 3.4 Process validation purpose statements.

It is also recommended that the purpose of each qualification—IQ, OQ, PQ, and PPQ—be adequately defined in the process validation procedure. Examples of each of these purpose statements can be found in Figure 3.4.

Sample Size Rationale

The sample size selected should be premised on the process risk index and the data type being considered (variable versus attribute). However, regardless of the data type or sample size selected premised on risk, written rationale for the sample size selected must be incorporated into each validation protocol (see Chapter 9).

Additionally, samples included in a validation should be obtained from lot(s) representative of production. The validation data collected from these samples will be used to demonstrate reproducibility and provide an accurate measure of variability for the processes being qualified.

Data Collection, Statistical Methodology, and Analysis

Data collection is a fundamental requirement of process validation; however, the application of statistical methodologies needed to ascertain whether the results of process validation are acceptable is the goal. The statistical methods employed to analyze the data collected shall be described within the protocol. Statistical analysis can be performed manually or with spreadsheets or software. If needed, results/specification data can be transformed to a normal distribution prior to the application of these statistical methods.

Handling Deviations

In a perfect world, process validations are flawlessly executed, with no anomalies or deviations noted. However, in the real world, deviations, although not necessarily routine, will occur during testing. When deviations occur as part of process validation, a formal investigation is required to ascertain whether the deviation is an outlier or material to the process validation results. Deviations should be fully discussed in the validation report and closed prior to accepting the validation. Additionally, deviations may result in repeating a portion of the process validation or the entire validation.

Validation Report

Once all of the validation activities are completed, the validation report will be generated. The purpose of the validation report is to summarize the testing results. The report should present conclusions premised on the data collected and the application of statistics employed to ascertain whether the process validation testing was successful. Two of the most important features of a validation report are a clear statement expressing that the validation either passed or failed, and what constitutes the need for repeating the validation.

For example:

> This validation was executed with no deviations reported and successfully met the acceptance criteria, thereby providing objective evidence that the process is capable of consistently meeting specified requirements. Revalidation is required if there is a significant process change, process improvement, design change, negative trends, if the intended purpose defined in the validation plan has changed, or within a specified interval (three years or 1m cycles).

Process Monitoring

Once a process has been successfully validated, the process shall be monitored and controlled to ensure that the process has not drifted and that specifications continue to be met (see Chapter 10). Monitoring of the process may be accomplished by one or more of the following, but is not limited to these items:

- Periodic destructive testing of subassemblies/final assemblies
- Lot release testing of a sample of subassemblies/final assemblies
- The ongoing review of performance data collected during manufacturing operations including the use of control charts
- Monitoring NCRs and complaint data

Revalidation Requirements

The requirements for revalidation should be part of the validation procedure. An example of revalidation requirements could be stated as "Revalidation will be performed when there is a significant process change impacting product performance or quality or when recurring process nonconformances necessitate a change to the process." If there is a decision made to not repeat process validation, written rationale will be required that documents the decision-making process.

3.5 SUMMARY

Writing effective policies and procedures in support of process validation requires a multidisciplinary team approach including representatives from quality, operations, and engineering. Although there are a variety of approaches, the six-step method can easily be employed for writing policy statements. When writing procedure, it is imperative that other procedures that affect process validation be considered. Procedures such as calibration/metrology, test method validation, and training are of immense importance. The content of the process validation procedure should include (a) purpose statement, (b) scope statement, (c) definitions, (d) references (internal and external), (e) responsibilities, (f) validation requirements (acceptance criteria), (g) a process flow, (h) sample size rationale, (i) data collection, statistical methodology, and analysis, (j) handling deviations, (k) validation report, and (l) process monitoring. Remember that although the collection of data is important, it is the subsequent application of statistical methodologies that is used to determine whether the process validation passed or failed. The validation report should always have a definitive statement of pass or fail and requirements for revalidation activities.

4
Validation Prerequisites

It is not possible to simply jump into a process validation effort without first understanding all of the potential influences that can impact the outcome of the validation of a process. There are multiple process validation prerequisites that need to be considered prior to an engineer typing that initial keystroke into the computer and commencing with the writing of the validation protocol. For example:

- Design of experiments
- Understanding the importance of calibration and metrology
- Ensuring that test method validation activities have been completed
- Ensuring that an adequate level of training has been attained for process validation engineers, reviewers, approvers, technicians, operators, and so on
- Third-party service providers executing validation protocols

Additionally, depending on the process validation being pursued, extensive planning may be needed when third-party service providers are required for package testing, sterilization validation, or some other specialized testing. Furthermore, there may be regulatory considerations when decisions are made to repeat process validation or process verification activities because of process changes, including materials, test methods, critical subcontractors or crucial suppliers, and changes to standards. Finally, repeated attempts at process validation, resulting in process validation failures, may result in potential design changes, equipment changes, procedural changes, material changes, or even supplier changes.

4.1 DESIGN OF EXPERIMENTS

One of the best definitions for *design of experiments* (DOE) is by K. Sundararajan (2015), retrieved from the isixsigma.com website: "Design of experiments (DOE) is a systematic method to determine the relationship between factors affecting a process and the output of that process. In other words, it is used to find cause-and-effect relationships. This information is needed to manage process inputs in order to optimize the output." In other words, critical process parameters (CPP) are the inputs and critical to quality (CTQ) attributes are the outputs.

Similarly to prerequisite requirements associated with process validation, some inherent knowledge of statistical tools and methodologies and an understanding of basic experimentation concepts are necessary to grasp a working-knowledge level of DOE. Granted, there are a plethora of software tools to assist with the creation and practical application of DOE. However, it is imperative that individuals conducting DOEs understand basic DOE concepts to ensure that the practical application of DOE is being appropriately employed (Sundararajan 2015).

Additionally, there are terms that are routinely employed as part of DOE studies. According to Sundararajan (2015), these terms include (a) controllable input factors, (b) uncontrollable input factors, (c) responses, (d) hypothesis testing, (e) blocking and replication, and (f) interaction. Definitions for these terms include:

- *Controllable input factors.* Categorized as input parameters that are capable of being modified in an experiment or process (Sundararajan 2015).

- *Uncontrollable input factors.* Categorized as parameters that cannot be changed. Note: These factors need to be recognized to understand how they may affect the response (Sundararajan 2015).

- *Responses or output measures.* Categorized as elements of the process outcome that gauge the desired effect (Sundararajan 2015).

- *Hypothesis testing.* Employed to determine the significant factors using statistical methods. There are two possibilities associated with a stated hypothesis statement: (a) the null hypothesis statement, and (b) the alternative hypothesis statement (Table 4.1). The null hypothesis statement is considered valid when the status quo is determined to be true. The alternative hypothesis statement is considered to be valid if the status quo is determined not to be true. Testing is performed at a level of significance that is premised on a probability (Sundararajan 2015).

- *Blocking and replication.* An experimental technique employed to identify and, hopefully, avoid unwanted variations in the input influencing the experimentation process. For example, an experiment may be conducted with the same equipment to avoid any equipment variations. Practitioners also replicate experiments, performing the same combination run more than once, in order to get an estimate of the total amount of random error that could influence a process (Sundararajan 2015).

- *Interaction.* When an experiment has three or more variables, an interaction is a situation in which the simultaneous influence of two variables on a third variable is not considered additive (Sundararajan 2015).

Figure 4.1 depicts the controllable and uncontrollable independent inputs (X's) and the dependent or response outputs (Y's). As can be seen in Figure 4.1, the inputs can be materials, methods, measurements, machines, people, and the environment.

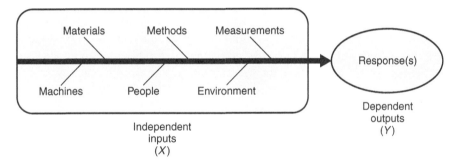

Figure 4.1 Cause-and-effect diagram depicting inputs (X's) and outputs (Y's).
Source: M. A. Durivage. 2016. *Practical Design of Experiments (DOE)*. Milwaukee: ASQ Quality Press. Used with permission.

Table 4.1 Hypothesis truth table.

Decision on null hypothesis	Null hypothesis is true	Null hypothesis is false
Accept (Fail to reject)	Correct decision Probability = $1-\alpha$	Type II error Probability = β
Reject	Type I error Probability = α	Correct decision Probability = $1-\beta$

Source: M. A. Durivage. 2014. *Practical Engineering, Process, and Reliability Statistics*. Milwaukee: ASQ Quality Press. Used with permission.

4.2 UNDERSTANDING THE IMPORTANCE OF CALIBRATION/METROLOGY

It is imperative that the measuring and monitoring equipment employed in support of process validation be capable of providing accurate and repeatable measurement results. The employment of well-documented calibration procedures, supported by capable measuring and monitoring equipment that is calibrated by a competent metrology service, is the cornerstone needed to support process validation. Although not a fundamental requirement, it is difficult to separate ISO/IEC 17025:2005 requirements from the selection of a qualified metrology service. However, considering the significant importance associated with accurate measurements, the underlying question needs to be "Why assume the risk associated with partnering with a metrology service that is not properly accredited?"

According to the World Meteorological Organization, the definition for the term "*metrology*" is *the science of measurement*. Additionally, metrology includes all aspects both theoretical and practical with reference to measurements, whatever their uncertainty, and in whatever fields of science or technology they occur (Duvernoy and Dubois 2006). Practitioners of process validation agree that there must be some inherent understanding of the importance of calibration and calibration methodologies to ensure that the application of calibration requirements is appropriate for the level of process validation being pursued. As delineated within a United Nations Industrial Development Organization (UNIDO) working paper published in 2006 entitled "Role of Measurement and Calibration in the Manufacture of Products for the Global Market: A Guide for Small and Medium-Sized Enterprises," ISO has defined *calibration* as "*the set of operations that establish, under specified conditions, the relationship between values indicated by a measuring instrument, a measuring system or values represented by a material measure, and the corresponding known values of a measurand.*"

Another concept requiring a basic level of comprehension is the influence of the term "*traceability*" on calibration. According to the UNIDO working paper, "*Traceability is the concept of establishing valid calibration of a measuring standard or instrument by step-by-step comparison with better standards up to an accepted national or international standard*" (UNIDO 2006). In the United States, the traceability requirement is linked directly to the National Institute of Standards and Technology (NIST).

According to Graeme C. Payne (2005), "*Calibration is essentially a process of comparison. An instrument is used to measure or is measured by a calibration standard, and the result is compared to two things: the known value and uncertainty of the standard and the performance specifications required by the customer.*" Additionally, the concept of calibration, through the comparison process, is relatively simple; however, the devil is in the details. Some of the details that need to be considered are the:

- "Assigned value of the measurement standard, which is usually determined from its calibration history;

- Known uncertainty of the standard, which comes from several places, including the historical reports of calibration and the internal statistical process control (SPC) methods many calibration labs have for their measurement systems. Labs that have an effective measurement SPC system know how their systems perform in that location, so their uncertainty values are likely to be more realistic—not always better, just more realistic;

- Environment of the calibration activity, which almost always includes temperature and relative humidity. Depending on the measurement, other influences such as absolute barometric pressure, the local gravitational vector, electromagnetic fields or building vibration may also have measurable effects;

- Methods and equipment used to make the comparisons; and

- Uncertainty of the measurement system relative to the published performance specifications of the item being calibrated or the customer's requirements, if different" (Payne 2005).

4.3 ENSURING THAT TEST METHOD VALIDATION (TMV) ACTIVITIES HAVE BEEN COMPLETED

According to a Eurolab Report written in 1996, "the definition used for *validation* in the ISO 8402 standard is 'confirmation by examination and provision of objective evidence that the particular requirements for a specific intended use are fulfilled.'" However, this definition infers that there is some stability in a validation process, but this stability is not necessarily true as there is significant variability in the TMV process. Figure 4.2 depicts the components of observed process variation comprising actual process variation and measurement variation. This variability is driven in part by the specific nature of the TMV target and the perceived flexibility some organizations pursue in developing TMVs. In fact, the perceived flexible nature of TMV can influence standard and nonstandard test methods. Regardless, the objective of TMV is to demonstrate that a TMV is appropriate for its intended purpose and that the decisions made are premised on the employment of measuring and monitoring capable of providing accurate, reproducible, and repeatable results. Simply stated, the goal of TMV is to demonstrate the suitability of the method through the use of appropriate scientific rationale.

When establishing a procedure for TMV, there are three categories of factors that are capable of influencing TMV results and measurement uncertainty:

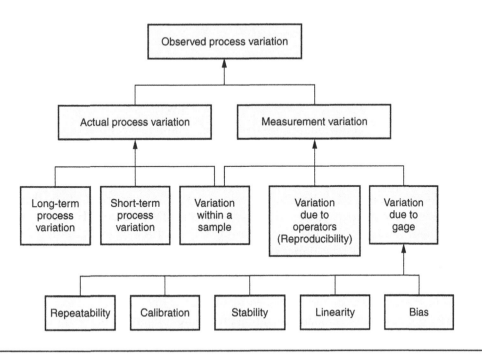

Figure 4.2   Possible sources of process variation.
Source: M. A. Durivage. 2016. *Practical Design of Experiments (DOE)*. Milwaukee: ASQ Quality Press. Used with permission.

- Instrumental and technical factors (sampling, homogeneity, test method, and equipment)
- Human factors
- Environmental factors

When developing the validation process for a test method, it is imperative that these three factors be adequately addressed as part of the TMV process. It is also imperative that an appropriate statistical methodology be identified to ensure that the results of TMV are adequately quantified through the employment of statistics. Although costs associated with TMV are always a concern with most organizations, the real focus needs to be on the actual TMV and the identification of the expected or required uncertainty of the test results and their intended use. Failure to properly execute a TMV or incorrectly specify the parameters for a TMV can quickly result in the exacerbation of unplanned quality costs driven by the manufacturing and acceptance of nonconforming product.

Instrumental and technical factors are directly related to the performance parameters of the test and measurement equipment employed in support of TMV. As previously mentioned, other influences include (a) sampling and the sample size selected, (b) the actual preparation of samples, and (c) test object homogeneity. The effect of these influences can be mitigated through the employment of the following provisions:

- Ensuring that references to internal procedures and external standards are made in the TMV (as appropriate)
- Precise definition of the equipment
- Development of a clear and concise description of the test procedure, including the operational parameters for the equipment
- Establishment of procedures for operational control and calibration
- The employment of SI units (when applicable traceability of measurements is required)

Human factors are related to the general competence of the technical staff and their ability to script TMV protocols and adequately execute TMV protocols. Human resources organizations are typically tasked with writing job descriptions that accurately reflect education, training, skills, and experience. In fact, ISO 9001 and ISO 13485 delineate the competence, awareness, and training requirements. The expectation is that organizations also provide some level of training, as appropriate. Additionally, qualifications required for each TMV should be placed into the actual procedure or clearly be specified in an organization's standard operating procedure (preferably in the training procedure or TMV procedure).

Environmental factors are associated with the environment where the actual TMV is being performed. The potential influence of the following parameters will need to be assessed and their impact controlled (Eurolab 1996):

- Atmospheric conditions where the TMV is going to be performed (temperature, pressure, and relative humidity)
- Pollution/contamination and the need to perform TMV in a *controlled environment room* (CER)
- Other environmental influences such as *electron magnetic interference* (EMI)

Finally, when developing the approach for TMV, two methodologies need to be considered: the "scientific approach" and the "comparative approach." The scientific approach employs the assessment of the representativeness, repeatability, and reproducibility of the TMV.

The *scientific approach* is pursued with references made to the different constitutive elements and features. Evidence of compliance should describe the representativeness of the selected properties and the associated uncertainty. The scientific approach can be premised on information published in relevant scientific and technical literature or on ad hoc investigations performed by the laboratory or organization developing the TMV. Regardless of who is developing the TMV, they must demonstrate that relevant factors (instrumental and technical, human, environmental) influencing the method have been analyzed and that they are under control within the uncertainty associated with the method (Eurolab 1996).

The *comparative approach* is pursued when the TMV is assessed by comparing its results to those obtained by means of another already validated test method that has been developed for the same purposes. When this type of comparison is not realistically possible, the performance characteristics of the TMV can be assessed through inter-laboratory comparisons. The results of a TMV are deemed to be "valid" when the results obtained from different laboratories fall within the expected uncertainty limit (Eurolab 1996).

One final point that needs to be made pertains to what many establishments view as the proverbial "off-the-shelf" methods available to industry. For example, when performing medical device package testing in accordance with ISO 11607-1:2009, options for test methods are depicted in Annexes B and C. However, the expectation is that establishments validate the use of these test methods with their own equipment and operators (Allen 2009). Additionally, the expectation is to ensure that third-party test facilities validate the use of these test methods before they commence with any testing activities.

4.4 TRAINING

A successful training program results in all members of an organization developing the appropriate skills and knowledge necessary to execute day-to-day activities needed to support operations, regardless of industry. Training programs developed by an organization really do need to be created with specific end goals as the target for success.

For example, basic training programs in the medical device industry are premised on providing a basic understanding of statutory and regulatory requirements and the application of standards, policies, procedures, and work instructions specific to an employee's job function. Granted, engineers and similar technical positions come with the expectation that the organizational member has completed some level of formal education or trade school; however, on-the-job training is still a salient requirement for key positions, including training required in support of process validation.

When writing a training procedure, there are associated fundamental elements that need to be considered:

- Basic training program requirements
- New employee orientation
- Quality management system training
- Career development training
- Training methodology
- Documentation of training

Basic Training Program Requirements

As with any training program, all employees are ultimately responsible for ensuring that their training is current and up-to-date. One of the tools that can be quickly developed and deployed is a *training matrix*. The training matrix can be created premised on a specific job function versus procedural requirements, or for smaller organizations, contain the employee's name. However, employees tasked with manufacturing duties may be required to exhibit some level of competence and product awareness (including defects) upon successful completion of training. To meet regulatory and statutory requirements, employees, contractors, temporary employees, and certain suppliers (as appropriate) should be included in the training program. Additionally, mandatory job descriptions should be a requirement, and the use of individual employee training plans is strongly recommended.

New Employee Orientation

It is imperative that a training program have a basic requirement for new employee orientation. It is recommended that this initial training occur immediately. The hiring managers should work with human resources to ensure that all new hires receive this training. Additionally, hiring managers should be responsible for preparing the appropriate documentation for all new hires, for example, a training plan.

Quality Management System Training

As part of the new employee orientation, *quality management system* (QMS) training should be provided for all of an organization's new employees. The training should provide sufficient information pertaining to the QMS and applicable statutory and regulatory requirements. Periodic retraining (recommend annually) on the QMS shall be conducted as needed for all employees. The source document for the retraining should be the organization's quality manual and subsidiary procedures. Periodic retraining should be premised on changes or modifications to the following:

- Significant changes to the QMS, quality policy manual, or procedures
- Quality policy and objectives
- International quality standards (for example, ISO 9001 and ISO 13485)
- Regulatory and statutory requirements

Additionally, the FDA requires that personnel who perform verification and validation activities shall be made aware of defects and errors that may be encountered as part of their job functions.

Career Development Training

Training and development plans are tools used to increase an employee's career development. Examples of this training are seminar courses, university classes, or internal cross-training. Employees and their managers are responsible for their professional development. However, in support of retaining key organizational members, building a strong career development program should be considered a mission-critical goal of any high-performing organization.

Training Methodology

There are several recognized methods of training: (a) self-training, (b) group training, and (c) on-the-job-training (OJT). *Self-training* consists of the self-study of a document, procedure, or work instruction, and certification by the individual that the document was read and all aspects of the document were clearly understood. Self-training is a viable method for most employees. However, training relating to product manufacturing, inspection, and product testing will be better served by the OJT methodology.

A qualified individual is required to conduct *group training*. Qualified individuals include originators of documents/revisions, those previously trained on a document revision, or individuals who have demonstrated a proficiency in the subject matter.

On-the job training is typically used to demonstrate an acceptable practice or processes. Where a document exists relevant to the content of the OJT training, the document can be employed to conduct the training. All OJT trainers should have documented evidence of completed training or competence in the subject matter taught.

Documentation of Training

All training activities are required to be documented. In a highly regulated industry, such as the medical device industry, regulators will ask to see training records in support of determining compliance with applicable regulatory and statutory requirements. In some cases, training records may be retained electronically through the use of a computerized data management system. The responsibility for managing training records may also be shared between managers and Human Resources or given to one organization for management, for example, the quality organization.

4.5 THIRD-PARTY SERVICE PROVIDERS

As mentioned earlier in this chapter, the importance of calibration/metrology cannot be overstated. The metrology resource selected to support an establishment's calibration needs must be appropriately qualified. The global standard for accreditation is ISO/IEC 17025:2005. If the metrology service selected does not possess an ISO/IEC 17025:2005 accreditation from a recognized authority, the risk of placing calibration business with an unaccredited laboratory is just too high.

The same oversight holds true for other third-party service providers. If an external source is being used to perform product testing, validation and verification activities, failure investigations, product sterilization, biocompatibility testing, and so on, the expectation is that these third-party service providers be appropriately qualified. In many cases, an ISO 9001, ISO 13485, or AS9100 certification from a recognized notified body or registrar will suffice. If the resources exist, it may also be practical to perform a supplier assessment to substantiate a service provider's ability to perform contracted activities in accordance with applicable standards, procedures, protocols, and validated test methods.

4.6 SUMMARY

It is not possible to perform process validation without first identifying and accounting for validation prerequisites: (a) design of experiments, (b) understanding the importance of calibration and metrology, (c) ensuring that test method validation activities have been completed, (d) ensuring that an adequate level of training has been attained for process validation engineers, reviewers, approvers, technicians, operators, and so on, and (e) third-party service providers executing validation protocols. Although each of these five prerequisites has its own fundamental purpose needed to strengthen an organization's approach to process validation, it is really not possible to successfully pursue PV without a basic understanding of each of these elements. DOE, metrology, TMV, training, and the use of third-party service providers allow organizations to create the necessary foundation for a rock-solid approach to process validation. However, removing any one of the prerequisites will weaken an organization's approach to PV. Before contemplating the writing and execution of a PV protocol, establishments must first ensure that all of the required prerequisites are adequately addressed either in the quality management system or a stand-alone procedure/work instruction.

5
Process Validation Considerations

Before attempting to begin process validation (PV) work, it is imperative that technical, procedural, operational, and risk (product and user) considerations are appropriately explored in terms of the process validation activities to be performed. The requirements for installation qualification (IQ), operational qualification (OQ), performance qualification (PQ), and process performance qualification (PPQ) will vary. In fact, risk will drive everything from sample size selection rationale to process-related variables requiring consideration. One simple fact that needs to be considered prior to launching any PV activity is that all production processes utilized in commercialized product, including reprocessing, must be evaluated to determine whether validation is necessary premised on two considerations: (1) Is the process output verifiable?, and (2) If the process output is verifiable, will it be sufficient and cost-effective? This chapter will explore PV considerations relevant to pursuing and successfully completing PV.

5.1 VALIDATION OR VERIFICATION

One of the more difficult questions medical device establishments find themselves asking is "When is PV actually required?" The good news is that 21 CFR, Part 820.75 clearly spells out the requirements. The FDA will hold device establishments accountable during inspections and even during the review of regulatory submissions, 510(k)s, and PMAs for compliance with PV requirements. It is better for establishments to take their time and effectively plan each PV effort versus pursuing an ad hoc approach that will have FDA questioning the general robustness of the validation effort.

21 CFR, Part 820, Section 820.75—Process Validation

(a) Where the results of a process cannot be fully verified by subsequent inspection and test, the process shall be validated with a high degree of assurance and approved according to established procedures. The validation activities and results, including the date and signature of the individual(s) approving the validation and where appropriate the major equipment validated, shall be documented.

(b) Each manufacturer shall establish and maintain procedures for monitoring and control of process parameters for validated processes to ensure that the specified requirements continue to be met.

(1) Each manufacturer shall ensure that validated processes are performed by qualified individual(s).

(2) For validated processes, the monitoring and control methods and data, the date performed, and, where appropriate, the individual(s) performing the process or the major equipment used shall be documented.

(c) When changes or process deviations occur, the manufacturer shall review and evaluate the process and perform revalidation where appropriate. These activities shall be documented.

5.2 PROCESS VALIDATION PLANNING

It is recommended that a *process failure mode and effects analysis* (PFMEA) be thoroughly vetted, as an important PV consideration, prior to the release of the *validation master plan* (VMP). The initial risk indices ascertained from the PFMEA can be employed to determine the sample size requirements for each process prior to undertaking PV. It should be noted that during the design and development process, a VMP is routinely pursued as part of the normal product development cycle. The VMP and PFMEA will consist of a listing of all production processes performed, including processes executed by third-party suppliers (for example, hydrophilic coating, sterilization, outsourced processes, and contract manufacturers) that affect product quality. If validation activities are performed by a contract manufacturer, then the VMP created by the contract manufacturer can be employed in place of an internally generated VMP and be used to track validation activities.

5.3 PROCESS SCOPING

Processes should be thoroughly developed, evaluated, and characterized. Considerations include but are not limited to:

- Process parameter development
- Sources of variation
- Detectability of variation
- Control of variation
- Tolerance stack analysis

Scoping studies should be performed prior to executing PV protocols. Equipment setup, process parameters, and processing duration should be evaluated. The use of statistically valid techniques (for example, design of experiments) can be used to establish key process parameters and/or for establishing process optimization. Scoping studies can also be documented as "lab notebook" studies such that they can be referenced in the PV protocols.

5.4 INSTALLATION QUALIFICATION

Installation qualification (IQ) establishes, by objective evidence, that all key aspects of the process equipment and ancillary system installations adhere to the manufacturer's approved specification and that the recommendations of the supplier of the equipment are suitably considered. Additionally, IQ determines, through documented evidence, that all systems and equipment are installed correctly. Considerations for the IQ should include, where applicable:

- Equipment description and design features
- Verification of correct start-up sequence
- Verification of correct setup parameters (hardware, firmware, and so on)
- Verification of calibration, preventive maintenance, and/or equipment cleaning schedules
- Verification of critical components and product features that could affect the process/product
- Verification of and reference to documentation such as drawings, manuals, and/or software documentation
- Verification that the required utilities are being supplied (voltage, air pressure, liquid nitrogen, and so on)
- Verification of spare parts list and functional sequences for machine operation
- Verification that specified and appropriate safety features are in place
- Verification that environmental requirements have been achieved for proper equipment operating conditions, including humidity, temperature, and so on
- Verification that installation facility requirements have been met (wiring, utilities, breaker, venting, and so on)
- All equipment/fixtures used in the process being validated must be considered

5.5 OPERATIONAL QUALIFICATION

Operational qualification (OQ) establishes, by objective evidence, that the equipment process control limits meet all predetermined requirements by challenging the limits to provide evidence that the predetermined process output requirements can meet the predetermined requirements. Additionally, OQ determines, through documented evidence, that the equipment process control limits meet all predetermined requirements. OQ also challenges the process parameters (often referred to as *limits testing* or *worst-case testing*) to make sure they result in a product that meets all defined requirements under all anticipated conditions of manufacturing. For OQ, sample size selection will be premised on the initial process risk index and data type (variable/attribute). A minimum sample size of eleven ($n = 11$) is recommended for variables data.

Equipment

Considerations for the OQ related to equipment should include, where applicable:

- Verification that controls (for example, buttons, switches) and safety features function as specified
- Equipment operator's manual
- Control of equipment throughout specified range (for example, maintain temperature minimum/maximum over time)
- Verification that software uses functions as specified (inputs/outputs, executes sequence of events reliably)
- Post-repair cleaning and calibration requirements

Process

Considerations for the OQ related to process should include, where applicable:

- Process control limits (for example, time, pressure, temperature, speed)
- Effects of sterilization and resterilization
- Environmental impact (for example, particulate generation, lubricants)
- Environmental conditions (for example, temperature, humidity)
- Software parameters
- Material handling requirements
- Operator training to a redlined or released manufacturing process instruction (MPI)

- Short-term process stability/capability studies (for example, latitude studies, control charts)

5.6 PERFORMANCE QUALIFICATION

Performance qualification (PQ) establishes, by objective evidence, that a process consistently produces a result and/or product that meets the predetermined requirements (reproducible and repeatable). Additionally, the objective of PQ is to demonstrate that the process will consistently produce acceptable product under normal operating conditions. Furthermore, PQ testing should always take place at nominal process conditions. Moreover, PQ samples should always be taken from product lot(s) representative of production, such that data generated from these samples will be able to demonstrate reproducibility and provide an accurate measure of variability for the processes being qualified. Sample size selection will be premised on the initial process risk index and data type (variable/attribute). Considerations associated with the PQ related to the process should include, where applicable:

- Environmental conditions (for example, temperature, humidity).
- Build day and operators involved in the build.
- Different material lots should be used among the different validation runs, if possible.
- Raw materials employed in the qualification run(s) should be sufficiently characterized (including the qualification of suppliers).
- Equipment setup during building of the test samples.
- Equipment setup of the test equipment.

5.7 PROCESS PERFORMANCE QUALIFICATION

Process performance qualification (PPQ) is the collection and evaluation of data, from the process design stage through commercialization, that establish scientific evidence that a process is capable of consistently delivering quality products. Additionally, the object of PPQ is to demonstrate that all validated manufacturing processes produce finished product that meets the product specifications. PPQ looks at an entire manufacturing process versus a single process. Complete product configurations are built in accordance with nominal process conditions. In support of PPQ, samples should be taken from lot(s) representative of production such that data generated in accordance with the PPQ protocol affirm that all significant variables of the entire manufacturing process being challenged are in a state of control at the time of the PPQ. Sample size selection will be premised on the initial process risk index and data type (variable/attribute).

5.8 STATISTICAL METHODS FOR DATA COLLECTION AND ANALYSIS

Statistical methods intended to be used to analyze the results should be clearly defined in the PV protocol. Statistical analysis can be performed manually, or using spreadsheets or software.

If needed, results and specification data can be transformed to a normal distribution prior to use of statistical methods, or a nonparametric analysis could be employed in support of data analysis.

5.9 PROCESS VALIDATION REPORTING

A master validation report (MVR) should be generated and considered the targeted output following completion of the process validations. This report should summarize and reference all protocols and results. It should derive conclusions regarding the validation status of the process.

5.10 PROCESS MONITORING

Once a process is validated, it must be monitored and controlled to ensure that the process has not drifted and that specifications will continue to be met. Monitoring of the process may be accomplished by one or more of the following methodologies, but is not limited to these:

- Process monitoring for specific processes using ongoing *process monitoring and lot-release testing*
- Verification activities in manufacturing process instructions (MPIs) or inspection instructions (IIs)
- Periodic destructive testing of subassemblies and final assemblies
- Lot release testing of a sample of subassemblies and final assemblies

5.11 DECISION TO REPEAT PROCESS VALIDATION

If any part of the process changes, the process should be evaluated to determine whether revalidation is required. Revalidation should be performed when there is a significant process change that could affect product performance or quality or when recurring process nonconformances necessitate a change to the process. If it is determined that revalidation is not required, the supporting justification for not performing validation should always be documented. Some processes should always be considered for revalidation even in the absence of a significant change (for example, annual EtO sterilization revalidation). Changes made to equipment (for example, equipment moved) should be evaluated if it is determined that the change will affect the process output. If this occurs, revalidation (for example, IQ/OQ) should always be performed.

5.12 CONCLUSION

One of the most important considerations associated with practical validation is validation planning. The initial planning, identification of scope, the equipment being employed as part of the validation, the operators, the materials selected for product manufacturing, calibration, and the use of third-party suppliers each play a significant role in achieving successful PV. It makes no difference whether the validation effort is focused on IQ, OQ, PQ, or PPQ; collectively, PV needs to be viewed as a sequential exercise. For example, OQ cannot be successfully completed without an acceptable IQ. PQ cannot be completed without an acceptable OQ, and so on. Each validation is in reality considered a building block for the next level of process validation. Finally, all potential PV influences, including the writing of a well-written protocol, supported by appropriate sample sizes, executed by trained operators and technicians, using calibrated measuring and monitoring equipment, with qualified materials, must always be considered before a serious attempt at process validation can be pursued. Otherwise, the achievability of reproducible and repeatable validation results is not possible.

6
Validation Master Plan

The *validation master plan* (VMP), or *master validation plan* (MVP), "serves as the validation roadmap, setting the course, justifying the strategy, out-lining the preliminary test and acceptance criteria, and documenting the necessary programs that ensure a continuing state of validation" (Saxton 2001). It is important to clearly define the intended purpose of the validation, which will aid in the determination of whether revalidation and retrospective validation activities are necessary. The main output of a VMP is a compilation of the process to be validated and associated documents with a schedule for revalidation and retrospective validation activities. The VMP should be developed and approved prior to the start of validation activities. The overall documentation hierarchy is shown in Figure 6.1.

Although not explicitly required by regulatory and certification bodies, the VMP is commonly requested by inspectors and auditors. In many ways, a VMP can be thought of as a calibration system for validations.

6.1 VALIDATION MASTER PLAN CONTENT

The content of the validation master plan as suggested by the Pharmaceutical Inspection Convention/Pharmaceutical Inspection Co-operation Scheme *Recommendations*

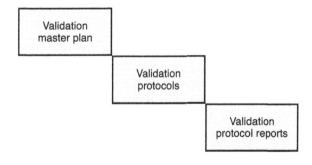

Figure 6.1 Validation documentation hierarchy.

on Validation Master Plan Installation and Operational Qualification Non-Sterile Process Validation Cleaning Validation (PI 006-3) is as follows:

- *Introduction.* This section provides a high-level overview of the validation strategy.

- *Organizational structure of all validation activities.* This section assigns the responsibility for determining the need, drafting the protocol, executing the protocol, and approvals.

- *Plant/process/product description.* This section provides the rationale for inclusion or exclusion for validation.

- *Specific process considerations.* This section should list any special requirements that may be necessary.

- *List of products/processes/systems to be validated.* This section includes a listing of all validation activities, including utilities, processes, and test method validations. Processes that are not validated should also be listed and marked *validation not required* (VNR) and appropriate rationale provided.

- *Key acceptance criteria.* The acceptance criteria for approving the validation protocols and reports.

- *Documentation format.* The formatting (including naming and numbering conventions) to be used for validation protocols and reports.

- *Required SOPs.* A list referencing the standard operating procedures (SOPs), work instructions (WIs), templates, and forms used for validation activities.

- *Planning and scheduling.* A schedule that depicts the requirements for validation, revalidation, and retrospective validations. This can be considered a "calibration" system for validations.

- *Change control.* The requirements for good documentation practices (GDPs), record storage, retention, and approvals.

Although the document is specifically designed for the operational qualification of nonsterile process validation cleaning validation, this format is well suited and easily adapted to any process requiring validation. The VMP can also be thought of as a "calibration" system for processes and should therefore contain a list of all validations. When not triggered by an event, the revalidation or retrospective validation intervals should be risk based. For example, high-risk validations, revalidation, or retrospective validation may be performed annually, a medium-risk validation every three years, and a low-risk validation every five years. An example master validation list including utilities, processes, and test method validations is shown in Table 6.1.

Table 6.1 Example master validation list.

Asset	Machine model	Process	Validation protocol	IQ	Risk	Validation date	Revalidation/ retrospective due date
#007	Sears	Plant compressed air	IQ-007-01	IQ	Low	Apr-13	Apr-18
#007	Sears	Plant compressed air	OQ-007-01	OQ	Low	Apr-13	Apr-18
#123	Acme	Op 1	IQ-123-01	IQ	High	Jun-15	Jun-16
#123	Acme	Op 1	OQ-123-01	OQ	High	Jun-15	Jun-16
#123	Acme	Op 1	PQ-123-01	PQ	High	Jun-15	Jun-16
#789	Generic	Op 4	IQ-789-01	IQ	Low	Dec-14	Dec-17
#789	Generic	Op 4	OQ-789-01	OQ	Low	Dec-14	Dec-17
#789	Generic	Op 4	PQ-789-01	PQ	Low	Dec-14	Dec-17
#345	Acme	Op 27	IQ-345-01	IQ	Med	Sep-14	Sep-17
#345	Acme	Op 27	OQ-345-01	OQ	Med	Sep-14	Sep-17
#345	Acme	Op 27	PQ-345-01	PQ	Med	Sep-14	Sep-17
#427	True	Op 15	TMV-427-01	TMV	High	Feb-14	Feb-15
N/A	N/A	Aseptic filling	PPQ-AF-02	PPQ	High	Jun-14	Jun-15

6.2 DETERMINING THE NEED FOR VALIDATION

The first item necessary in the development of a VMP is the determination of which processes must be validated and which processes can be fully verified. The process validation decision tree depicted in Figure 6.2 is a useful tool in making this evaluation.

Begin with box A: is the process output verifiable? If the answer is positive, then the consideration should be made as to whether or not verification alone is sufficient to eliminate unacceptable risk and is a cost-effective solution. Remember that 100% verification is generally only 80% effective.

Box B asks, is the verification sufficient and cost-effective? If yes, the output should be verified and the process should be appropriately controlled (box C). If the output of the process is not verifiable, then the decision should be to validate the process (box D). Alternatively, it may become apparent that the product or process should be redesigned to reduce variation and improve the product or process (box E). Also, a change in a manufacturing process may result in the need for process validation even though the process formerly only required verification and control. The risk or cost may also be reduced by redesigning the product or process to a point where simple verification is an acceptable decision (box E).

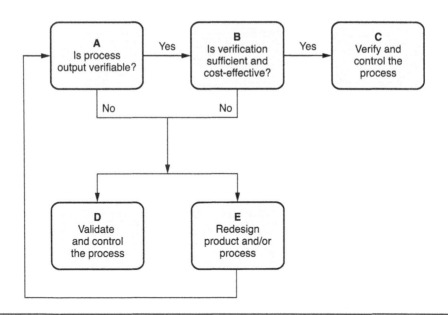

Figure 6.2 Process validation decision tree.
Source: Adapted from GHTF Study Group 3. 2004. *Quality Management Systems—Process Validation Guidance.* 2nd ed.

The following list from the from GHTF Study Group 3 *Quality Management Systems—Process Validation Guidance* (January 2004) provides examples of processes that (1) should be validated, (2) may be satisfactorily covered by verification, and (3) may be verifiable, but, for business purposes, validation can be chosen:

1. Processes that should be validated:
   - Sterilization processes
   - Cleanroom ambient conditions
   - Aseptic filling processes
   - Sterile packaging sealing processes
   - Lyophilization process
   - Heat-treating processes
   - Plating processes
   - Plastic injection molding processes

2. Processes that may be satisfactorily covered by verification:
   - Manual cutting processes
   - Testing for color, turbidity, total pH for solutions

- Visual inspection of printed circuit boards
- Manufacturing and testing of wiring harnesses

3. Processes for which the above model may be useful in determining the need for validation:
   - Certain cleaning processes
   - Certain human assembly processes
   - Numerical control cutting processes
   - Certain filling processes.

6.3 CONCLUSION

The validation master plan (VMP), or master validation plan (MVP), "serves as the validation roadmap, setting the course, justifying the strategy, out-lining the preliminary test and acceptance criteria, and documenting the necessary programs that ensure a continuing state of validation" (Saxton 2001). The main output of a VMP is a compilation of the process to be validated and associated documents with a schedule for revalidation and retrospective validation activities. Although not required by regulatory and certification bodies, the VMP is commonly requested by inspectors and auditors. In many ways, a VMP can be thought of as a "calibration system" for validations. When not triggered by an event, revalidation or retrospective validation activities should be risk based and clearly defined in the VMP.

7
Software Validation

The validation of software can be an extremely challenging endeavor for organizations to pursue. In many instances the software may be embedded into the controller (firmware) of a critical piece of measuring and monitoring equipment. Historically, when regulators questioned the application of software in measuring and monitoring equipment, or even software employed in a finished medical device, a canned answer such as "this is just a black box" was generally accepted. Unfortunately, that type of response is no longer accepted by the FDA or other regulators. In fact, if a device establishment submits a 510(k) or PMA to the FDA, and the device employs software, the agency is going to want to see all of the supporting documentation associated with the development of the software, including verification and validation activities. In accordance with 21 CFR, Section 820.30(g), "Design Validation," the Quality System Regulation (QSR) specifically delineates the requirement for validating software. A similar requirement is delineated within 21 CFR, Section 820.70(i), "Automated Processes." Additionally, Part 11 requirements must also be considered when pursuing software validation and the validation of computerized systems. Hopefully, considering the emphasis being placed on the validation of software by regulators and the intrinsic value of an effective approach to software validation, the information provided in this chapter will guide the reader to a better understanding of software validation.

7.1 FDA REQUIREMENTS FOR SOFTWARE VALIDATION

21 CFR, Section 820.30—Design Controls

(g) Design validation. Each manufacturer shall establish and maintain procedures for validating the device design. Design validation shall be performed under defined operating conditions on initial production units, lots, or batches, or their equivalents. Design validation shall ensure that devices conform to defined user needs and intended uses, and shall include testing of production units under actual or simulated use conditions. Design validation shall include software validation and risk analysis, where appropriate. The results of design validation, including identification of the design, method(s), the date, and the individual(s) performing the validation, shall be documented in the DHF.

21 CFR, Section 820.70—Production and Process Controls

(i) Automated processes. When computers or automated data processing systems are used as part of production or the quality system, the manufacturer shall validate computer software for its intended use according to an established protocol. All software changes shall be validated before approval and issuance. These validation activities and results shall be documented.

Note: Software validation also applies to programmable logic controllers (PLCs) and computer numerical control (CNC) machines.

21 CFR, Section 11—Electronic Records; Electronic Signatures

Section 11.1 Scope

"*(e)* Computer systems (including hardware and software), controls, and attendant documentation maintained under this part shall be readily available for, and subject to, FDA inspection.

Section 11.10 Controls for Closed Systems

(a) Validation of systems to ensure accuracy, reliability, consistent intended performance, and the ability to discern invalid or altered records.

7.2 DETERMINING THE NEED FOR SOFTWARE VALIDATION

The decision to pursue software validation is premised on multiple factors influencing all sizes of medical device establishments. The regulatory and statutory requirements should always top the list of factors. However, the driving force should always be the finished medical device safety and efficacy. Additional reasons include:

- Ensuring the quality and accuracy of software in its intended use
- Having the ability to provide documented evidence to a regulatory body reflecting that software was appropriately developed in a controlled environment
- Cost savings associated with developing the software correctly, the first time

Before diving into some of the essential requirements for software, a clear and concise definition for software validation needs to be understood. According to Process Pro (2013):

> Software validation confirms that certain specifications coincide with user needs, the software is meeting intended use, and requires objective evidence that the requirements can be consistently fulfilled. This is required for any company

covered by the Food, Drug, and Cosmetic Act and 21 CFR Parts 210 and 211. Also, if a company is keeping current good manufacturing practice (cGMP) data electronically and relying on that information to make cGMP decisions, they are required to perform software validation. Manufacturers who continue to see increased enforcement of these regulations include pharmaceutical, nutritional supplement, and cosmetic companies.

Additionally, according to Gregory Gogates (2012) there are three categories of software that require consideration when debating whether to pursue software validation:

- Commercial off-the shelf (COTS)
- Modified off-the-shelf (MOTS)
- Custom—also known as *written code*

COTS software is essentially procured on the open market with limited or no ability to modify the code. Typically, COTS software is procured for a specific purpose or for use in a dedicated environment such as with a measurement instrument. Examples of COTS software include Microsoft products such as Excel or Access, or software such as Minitab. However, when this type of software is employed in a regulated environment, it is imperative that the software be appropriately validated for its intended use. For example, if cells used in spreadsheets are preprogramed, once the formulas used are verified and validated, the cell should be locked. In fact, it is strongly recommended that procedural controls be written and implemented to assist in the management of COTS software. Additionally, firmware embedded inside measuring and monitoring equipment or automated processing equipment should be validated by the manufacturer prior to ever performing the initial installation qualification (IQ). However, it is never safe to assume that COTS software has been properly validated. It is imperative that establishments ask about the validation of software prior to purchasing equipment with "embedded software."

MOTS software implies that the software has been modified, tailored, or customized for a specific application (Gogates 2012). Examples of MOTS software include software employed for the control of metrology records, Lab Windows, data acquisition software, and software that has been tailored for the control of documents, for example, product data management (PDM). MOTS software requires validation. Additionally, functional areas where the code has been modified must be documented and the functional performance properly vetted.

Custom software is essentially proprietary code that has been written by a vendor for a specific application. Examples of custom software and development environments include JAVA, C++, SAP, and CATSWeb. Software in this category can be employed in a stand-alone application or be interfaced with other software and hardware modules and/or products. This software should be thoroughly validated for its intended use. Custom software should be developed in a controlled environment, employing product life cycle requirements similar to those defined in ISO/IEC 26550:2015.

7.3 SOFTWARE DEVELOPMENT LIFE CYCLE

The establishment of an effective software life cycle does not have to be overly burdensome. The typical software development cycle depicted in Figure 7.1 will be viewed from a macro level. A basic software development life cycle will contain five steps:

1. The requirements phase
2. The design and development phase
3. The software construction phase
4. The software testing phase (verification and validation)
5. The software release phase

Requirements Phase

During the requirements phase, the software functionality, intended use, safety, and user requirements are defined. The output of this initial phase is essential to the software requirements document.

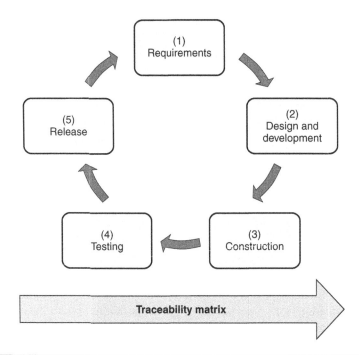

Figure 7.1 Software development life cycle phases.

Design and Development Phase

During this phase, the actual designing of the software—including logic flows, process maps, and state machine diagrams that reflect the interrelationships of the modules—is taking place. In an FDA-regulated environment, the expectation is that design reviews are performed at appropriate stages throughout the design and development process. It is strongly recommended that these reviews occur at the close of each design phase. The output of the design and development phase will be the software design document.

Software Construction Phase

During this phase, the software engineers begin writing and debugging the code. The code debugging work in this phase is not part of the verification and validation work. Rather, it is basic groundwork completed by the software engineers to ensure that the code functions and performs in its most fundamental manner on the way to meeting the software requirements and system functionality, without any gross crashes or deviations from its original designed logic. The output of the software construction phase is the actual source code and the compiled executable files.

Software Testing Phase

During the software testing phase, initial verification and validation testing of the software occurs. It is imperative that verification and validation protocols be written to guide the testing, including all of the individual test cases. Additionally, the test cases should be mapped back to the software requirements document. According to Gogates (2012), important influences requiring consideration during the software test phase are (a) the verification of math, (b) the identification of valid/invalid inputs, (c) the potential for power failure, (d) code walk-through requirements, and (e) structural and functional tests. Note: When software anomalies are identified (AKA software bugs), these bugs need to be thoroughly assessed and tracked until they are properly resolved.

Software Release Phase

In this phase the code is released for its intended use. In some cases the release may entail the formal integration of the software into a piece of hardware. When such integration occurs, additional validation activities are warranted.

Final Review of the Traceability Matrix

The traceability matrix captures documented evidence that the software design requirements are adequately mapped to the design and to the test cases performed. The traceability matrix is essentially a quality document that reflects that the software has been appropriately designed, developed, tested, integrated, and released.

7.4 CREATION OF THE USER REQUIREMENTS DOCUMENT

When creating the user requirements document, best practice is to initially create a list of short, clear, and concise requirements that delineate the targeted functionality of the software. According to Process Pro (2013), it is best to employ a documentation approach using short statements. Additionally, during this initial step, members of the software validation team can be identified. It is imperative that these team members participate during the initial brainstorming sessions so they can be well versed in the targeted software functionality and subsequent design review sessions. If the appropriate amount of time and effort is invested in the creation of the user requirements document, the output will help establishments make intelligent decisions when the procurement of software and products finally occurs.

7.5 DEVELOPMENT OF THE PROJECT PLAN— MASTER VALIDATION PLAN (MVP)

Similarly to any major project pursued by establishments, software validation will require a project plan. A well-defined project plan will identify (a) roles and responsibilities associated with the validation, (b) what is actually being validated, (c) where the validation will occur, and (d) when the validation will occur. The validation team will retain the responsibility for managing the entire software validation process. It is recommended that the following functional roles be considered for inclusion on the validation team:

- Project management
- Engineering (software, R&D, manufacturing, technicians, and so on)
- Quality assurance (QA/RA manager(s), engineers, inspectors, and document control)
- Operations (assemblers, material handlers, and so on)
- Regulatory affairs

It is imperative that the roles and responsibilities of the functional groups and/or individual validation team members be defined in the validation master plan (VMP). Additionally, the VMP should also include a system description, purpose, environment specifications, assumptions, exclusions, limitations, testing and acceptance criteria, error resolution, and system documentation (Process Pro 2013).

A decision must be made as to whether the software actually needs to be validated. Figures 7.2 and 7.3 provide examples of software validation decision trees.

Software Validation 55

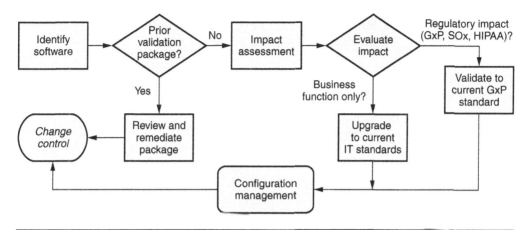

Figure 7.2 Software validation decision tree—legacy software.
Source: Courtesy of John English, HCCP of John T. English LLC—Systems/Regulatory Consulting.

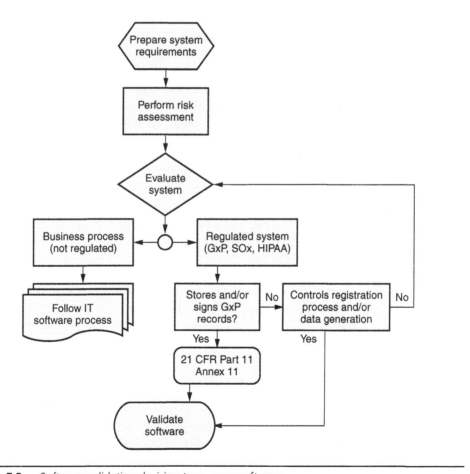

Figure 7.3 Software validation decision tree—new software.
Source: Courtesy of John English, HCCP of John T. English LLC—Systems/Regulatory Consulting.

7.6 CREATION OF THE FUNCTIONAL SPECIFICATIONS DOCUMENT

The functional specifications document is nothing more than an extension of the user requirements with additional granularity added. According to Process Pro (2013), the requirements are now expanded to three or four sentences to support the additional information added. Additionally, a link should be established between the user and functional requirements. This link will be needed to identify the initial test cases. Furthermore, the end result will be the creation of a traceability matrix that will allow the validation team to trace the test cases back to the requirements. Finally, the traceability matrix will be an invaluable tool for Quality in their final examination of the software validation results to ensure that all of the inputs and outputs have been adequately assessed.

7.7 PERFORMANCE OF THE GAP ANALYSIS

During the review of the functional specifications, a gap analysis is created (Process Pro 2013). The gap analysis is employed as a tool to assist the validation team in ascertaining risk. During the gap assessment, the difference between the desired or targeted performance versus the existing performance is assessed. All risks identified during the performance of the gap analysis should be documented and prioritized. Design, user, and process FMEAs become invaluable tools when assessing risk. In fact, EN ISO 14971:2012 requirements should be employed in support of implementing effective risk mitigation. Note: If a gap is identified as a "high risk," risk mitigation activities must be pursued.

7.8 WRITING OF THE INSTALLATION PROTOCOL

The installation protocol document will outline how the software should be installed. The actual installation is typically performed by an approved vendor unless the establishment is developing the software and hardware and performing the integration activities. At this stage of the validation process, installation and hardware specifications should have been written and released. Without written specifications it will not be possible to verify the performance of the software and/or hardware.

7.9 WRITING OF THE INSTALLATION REPORT

The installation report is a written summary supported by the compilation of information and documentation that attests to claims of proper installation. Simply stated, the written installation report is documented evidence of compliance. If a supplier is tasked with performing the installation, they will be tasked with providing the written installation report and documented evidence of compliance.

7.10 WRITING OF THE TESTING PROTOCOL(S)—VALIDATION PROTOCOLS

The testing protocols will contain the same essential requirements associated with normal process validation, such as the test cases, process equipment, sample size, risk index, confidence intervals, test methods, acceptance criteria, training, data collection sheets, test and inspection parameters, and so on. The goal of the protocols is to ensure that software is appropriately tested and validated for its intended use. If a third-party testing facility is employed, they should be provided with a copy of the validation protocol, or if the decision is made for the supplier to employ their own testing protocol(s), it is incumbent upon the establishment to review and approve the vendor-provided protocol(s). The protocols, when executed, will be used to collect and document objective evidence that the software validation was properly performed. The data gleaned during the execution of the test protocols will be employed in the writing of the final software validation report.

7.11 FINAL TEST REPORT

The final test report, also known as the *validation report*, contains the documented evidence that the software has been properly validated. The report shall contain:

- A copy of the protocol (for reference)
- Data collection sheets
- Training records
- Calibration records
- Protocol deviations
- Nonconformances noted (bugs, and the subsequent investigation performed)
- A definitive pass/fail statement
- A statement of what warrants a repeat of the validation
- A copy of the traceability matrix
- A signature page including the author and all of the reviews/approvers required by procedures

7.12 SYSTEM RELEASE/GO-LIVE

Once all of the testing (verification and validation) activities have been successfully completed, the system release allows the software to be used in production. According to Process Pro (2013), prior to the system release/go-live (a) the users must be trained, (b) data entered (as appropriate), and (c) business scenarios completed.

7.13 VALIDATION COMPLETION

Once the validation of software has been completed, the system shall be maintained in a validated state. Maintaining a validated state requires the writing of procedures for:

- Monitoring software performance
- Collecting and documenting performance issues (bugs)
- Mitigation of software performance issues (CAPA)
- Software change control
- The retaining of records

7.14 REPEATING VALIDATION

If any part of the software (code) changes, the changes should be evaluated to determine whether revalidation is required. Revalidation should be performed when there is a significant change to the software that could affect functionality, safety, performance, or quality.

If it is determined that revalidation is not required, supporting justification for not performing validation should always be documented.

7.15 SUMMARY

The validation of software does not have to be an overly challenging endeavor for establishments. If software is designed, developed, and tested in a controlled environment, and the individuals tasked with writing and executing the test protocols are appropriately trained, then software validation should be a relatively benign task. However, the FDA requires that software employed in finished medical devices or software employed in automated processes be appropriately validated. This regulatory oversight adds an additional level of complexity. Regardless, when well-written test scripts are properly executed and the results compiled into a clear and concise software validation report, the outcome of the validation project will be software capable of functioning correctly and safely in its intended use. Finally, if software has not been designed, developed, and tested in accordance with 21 CFR, Part 820 requirements, the associated regulatory risk will increase significantly.

8
Revalidation and Retrospective Validation

Revalidation and retrospective validation are part of on the ongoing process validation life cycle (see Figure 8.1). Retrospective validation is a validation activity that utilizes data from a stable process to formally document the review of the process, whereas revalidation requires the re-execution of a validation protocol due to a significant process change, process improvement, design change, if the intended purpose defined in the validation plan has changed, negative trends, or when triggered by a specified interval (time or cycles). Revalidation is generally better accepted and preferred over retrospective validations. The determination of retrospective validation and revalidation activities should be clearly defined and documented in a procedure, with the frequency of these activities being risk based. Additionally, the validation master plan (VMP), or master validation plan (MVP), should specify the frequency of a periodic review and/or the conditions necessary to trigger a retrospective validation or revalidation activity.

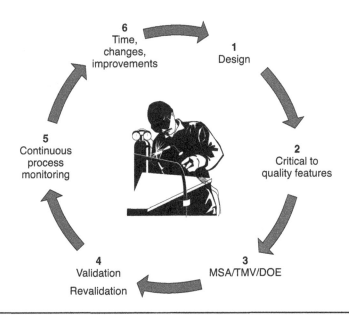

Figure 8.1 Typical process validation life cycle.

1. The process validation life cycle begins with the *design* phase, which includes design verification and design validation activities. During this phase, the product/process is investigated and the characteristics/attributes are defined.

2. The next step is to determine which characteristics/attributes are *critical to quality* (CtQ). CtQ characteristics/attributes are those characteristics/attributes that have been identified during design verification and design validation and risk management processes. The characteristics/attributes that are not QtC should be evaluated using a first article layout (FAL) or first article inspection (FAI) technique using 3–5 parts to demonstrate acceptability of the characteristics/attributes. This phase will determine which characteristics/attributes must be measured during the validation.

3. Prior to performing the validation, a *measurement systems analysis* (MSA), gage repeatability and reproducibility (GR&R) study, or *test method validation* (TMV) should be conducted to ensure that the measurement system is capable of assessing the characteristics/attributes being measured. The purpose of the *design of experiments* (DOE) is to determine which factors (inputs) and what levels affect the characteristics/attributes (outputs) of the parts being produced.

4. The next phase is the actual *validation* or *revalidation* activities. This step ensures that the process is capable of consistently producing within the design specifications previously validated through design verification and design validation.

5. Once the process is validated, the next phase is *continuous process monitoring*. This step verifies that the process is producing parts consistently. Continuous process monitoring typically uses control charts, process capability studies, and process yields to monitor the validated process.

6. The last phase of the process validation life cycle assesses the impact of *time*, *changes*, and *improvements* on the process and helps establish the revalidation or retrospective validation interval.

As mentioned earlier, the revalidation or retrospective validation interval should be risk based. If a significant change has occurred to the product design or a previously validated process, an assessment of the changes should be conducted to determine whether the change has had any adverse effect on product quality. If this is not the case, a risk-based rationale should be documented to establish an appropriate interval. For example, sterilization validations are usually revalidated annually, whereas an injection molding process may be evaluated every five years. The criteria for the revalidation/retrospective validation interval should be defined in a procedure and, where possible, related to the risk management documents, such as a failure mode and effects analysis (FMEA).

8.1 RETROSPECTIVE VALIDATION

Retrospective validation should only be conducted on stable processes that have demonstrated acceptable process capability. Additionally, the process being retrospectively validated should not have undergone any significant changes. The following items should be analyzed and evaluated for changes when performing a retrospective validation:

- Equipment
- Software
- Raw materials
- Nonconformances
- Complaints
- Maintenance records
- Packaging materials
- Facilities
- Operating parameters
- Continuous process monitoring
- Production yields
- Process capability studies

Because a retrospective validation is a historical review, data can be gleaned from representative batch records (including failed and/or reworked/reprocessed lots), complaint files, maintenance records, continuous process monitoring, control charts, process capability studies, scrap rates, and other relevant sources of data. Because this type of validation relies on historical data, the use of a retrospective validation is not the best choice for an initial validation and should only be used for an initial validation with significant documentation and justification. Any deviation from the approved protocol should be documented, investigated, closed, and approved prior to accepting the retrospective validation.

It is required that a statistically significant number of records be reviewed. It is suggested that records from 10 to 30 lots be collected and analyzed in order to demonstrate that the validated process in in a state of control. The number of records analyzed should be defined in the retrospective validation protocol.

Retrospective validations should be conducted by individuals that are appropriately qualified by a defined combination of experience, education, training, and certifications. Proper documentation that records the experience, education, training, and certifications is required. It is also important to ensure that the individuals performing the validation activities are trained on the validation procedure(s) and the actual validation plans, protocols, and reports.

The retrospective validation plans, protocols, reports, and deviations should be managed using change control and handled as any other quality record. These records should be legible and stored in a manner so as to minimize deterioration and to prevent loss. If these records are stored electronically, they should be backed up.

Revalidation is generally better accepted over retrospective validations by regulatory agencies. However, with proper documentation and justification, retrospective validations can be successfully defended during inspections and audits.

8.2 REVALIDATION

Revalidation is required when there is a significant change to a process. Revalidation provides objective evidence that changes in a process do not adversely affect product quality or that the process is performing as intended during the initial validation. Items that can trigger the need for a process to be revalidated include:

- Changes in equipment
- Changes in components (when like parts are not available or used)
- Changes in specifications
- Changes in the product risk profile
- Changes in the environmental conditions
- Changes in a supplier
- Changes in raw materials
- Changes in packaging components
- Changes in utilities
- Complaints
- Audits
- Maintenance records (planned and unplanned)
- Equipment location (within a facility)
- Plant relocation
- Unfavorable quality trend
- Changes in standard operating procedures (SOPs) and work instructions (WIs)
- Significant changes in personnel
- Process optimization/improvements

- Changes in regulatory standards and expectations
- Changes in certification requirements
- Time

Revalidation activities are generally easier to perform than the initial validation due to access and availability of the previous validation results and the documentation collected. It is very important when using the initial or revised protocol as the basis for revalidation that the protocol still complies with internal procedures, work instructions, and regulatory and certification requirements. Any deviation from the approved protocol should be documented, investigated, reviewed, approved, and closed prior to accepting the revalidation.

It may not be necessary to revalidate the installation qualification (IQ) and operational qualification (OQ) when the process has not changed. However, the performance qualification (PQ) and process performance qualification (PPQ) should be revalidated to demonstrate that the process is performing as intended during the initial validation.

As with retrospective validations, revalidations should be conducted by individuals that are appropriately qualified by a defined combination of experience, education, training, and certifications. Proper documentation that records the experience, education, training, and certifications is required. It is also important to ensure that the individuals performing the validation activities are trained on the validation procedure(s) and the actual validation plans, protocols, and reports.

Revalidation plans, protocols, reports, and deviations should be change controlled and handled as any other quality record. These records should be legible and stored so as to minimize deterioration and to prevent loss. If these records are stored electronically, they should be backed up.

8.3 CONCLUSION

Revalidation and retrospective validation are part of the ongoing process validation life cycle. Retrospective validation is a validation activity that utilizes data from a stable process to formally document the review of the process, whereas revalidation requires the re-execution of a validation protocol due to a significant process change, process improvement, or design change, or when triggered by a specified interval (time or cycles). Revalidation is generally better accepted and preferred over retrospective validations. The determination for conducting retrospective validation and revalidation activities should be clearly defined and documented in a procedure, with the frequency of these activities being risk based. Additionally, the validation master plan (VMP), or master validation plan (MVP), should specify the frequency of periodic review and/or the conditions necessary to trigger a retrospective validation or revalidation activity.

9
Sample Size Considerations

Probably the most frequent question related to process validation is "how many samples do I need?" This is a very complex question, and the answer is "it depends." The answer is dependent on many factors, but the most important consideration is patient and user risk driven by product safety and efficacy. When assessing health and safety considerations, one must utilize a risk-based approach in determining a sample size that is adequate and provides a defensible statistical significance.

The sample size will also depend on the type of data being collected: variable versus attribute. *Variables* data are measurements that are measured on a continuous scale, such as weight or length, whereas *attributes* data are premised on binary measurements: pass/fail, go/no-go. Where possible, the use of variables data is preferred, as this type of measurement provides much more statistical information with fewer samples (see Figure 9.1).

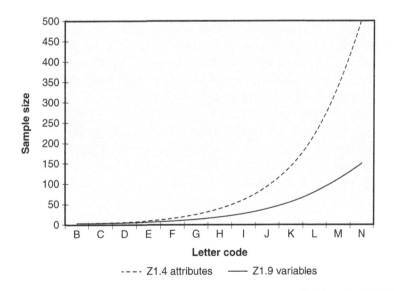

Figure 9.1 Comparison of variable and attribute sample sizes with equivalent protection.

9.1 SAMPLING PLAN STANDARDS

There are three primary recognized standards used for sampling:

1. ANSI/ASQ Z1.4–2003 (R2013) *Sampling Procedures and Tables for Inspection by Attributes* is an acceptance sampling system to be used with switching rules on a continuing stream of lots for acceptance quality limit (AQL) specified. It provides tightened, normal, and reduced plans to be applied for attributes inspection for percent nonconforming, or nonconformities per 100 units.

2. ANSI/ASQ Z1.9–2003 (R2013) *Sampling Procedures and Tables for Inspection by Variables for Percent Nonconforming* is an acceptance sampling system to be used on a continuing stream of lots for acceptance quality limit (AQL) specified. It provides tightened, normal, and reduced plans to be used on measurements that are normally distributed. Variation may be measured by sample standard deviation, sample range, or known standard deviation. It is applicable only when the normality of the measurements is assured.

3. ANSI/ASQC Q3-1988 *Sampling Procedures and Tables for Inspection of Isolated Lots by Attributes.* This acceptance sampling system is used when one or more lots that are isolated or separated from a continuous stream of lots are submitted for acceptance. The quality levels referenced in this standard are indexed by limiting quality.

An additional recognized "standard," *Zero Acceptance Number Sampling Plans (C = 0)*, a sampling plan by Nicholas Squeglia, is also widely accepted and used, especially within the FDA-regulated industries due to the plan's emphasis on consumer protection. The zero acceptance number plans developed by Squeglia were originally designed and used to provide equal or greater consumer protection with less overall inspection than the corresponding Z1.4 sampling plans. This "standard" provides a set of attribute plans for lot-by-lot inspection with the acceptance number in all cases as zero. $C = 0$ sampling plans are considered stand-alone sampling plans.

The question then becomes what acceptable quality level (AQL) should be used for ensuring a statically significant sample? The answer to this question will depend on the risk acceptance that the organization is willing to accept and defend. The AQL will also depend on the goods being produced. For example, consumer goods would probably require a different AQL than a high-risk medical device.

9.2 SAMPLE SIZE CALCULATION BASED ON CONFIDENCE AND RELIABILITY WITH ZERO FAILURES ALLOWED

There are often times when the question arises of how many samples are necessary to perform a test without a failure in order to demonstrate both confidence and reliability. The following formula can perform this calculation:

$$n = \frac{\ln(1-C)}{\ln(R)}$$

where

n = Sample size

C = Confidence level

R = Reliability

Example: What is the sample size required to perform a test without failure to be 95% confident the part is 99% reliable?

$$n = \frac{\ln(1-C)}{\ln(R)} = \frac{\ln(1-.95)}{\ln(.99)} = 298.07 \text{ (rounded up to the next integer, 299)}$$

To be 95% confident the part is 99% reliable, 299 parts must be tested without failure.

9.3 RELIABILITY ESTIMATE WHEN SAMPLE SIZE IS PROVIDED

When the sample is provided, and tests are performed without a failure, with a given confidence, we can calculate the reliability with the following formula:

$$R = (1-C)^{1/(n+1)}$$

where

n = Sample size

C = Confidence level

R = Reliability

Example: What is the reliability when tests were performed without failure using 32 samples, and we require 90% confidence?

$$R = (1-C)^{1/(n+1)} = (1-0.90)^{1/(32+1)} = .9326 \text{ or } 93.26\%$$

9.4 SAMPLE SIZE CALCULATION WITH FAILURES ALLOWED

There are often times when the question arises of how many samples are necessary to perform a test with r number of failures to demonstrate both confidence and reliability. The following formula can perform this calculation:

$$n = \frac{0.5 \times \chi^2_{(1-C, 2(r+1))}}{1-R}$$

where

n = Sample size

r = Number of failures

C = Confidence level

R = Reliability

$\chi^2_{(1-C, 2(r+1))}$ = Distribution of the chi-square value for a given confidence level for r degrees of freedom (see Appendix F, Distribution of the Chi-Square)

Example: What is the sample size required to ensure we are 90% confident that we are 90% reliable when three failures occur?

$$n = \frac{0.5 \times \chi^2_{(1-C, 2(r+1))}}{1-R} = \frac{0.5 \times \chi^2_{(1-0.90, 2(3+1))}}{1-R} = \frac{0.5 \times 13.362}{1-0.90} = 66.81$$

rounded up to the next whole integer, 67 samples are required

9.5 RELIABILITY ESTIMATE WHEN SAMPLE SIZES ARE SPECIFIED

When the sample is provided and tests are performed with r number of failures, with a given confidence, we can calculate the reliability with the following formula:

$$R = 1 - \frac{0.5 \times \chi^2_{(1-C, 2(r+1))}}{n}$$

where

n = Sample size

r = Number of failures

C = Confidence level

R = Reliability

$\chi^2_{(1-C, 2(r+1))}$ = Distribution of the chi-square value for a given confidence level for r degrees of freedom (see Appendix F, Distribution of the Chi-Square)

Example: What is the reliability necessary to ensure we are 90% confident when 69 samples are tested and three failures occur?

$$R = 1 - \frac{0.5 \times \chi^2_{(1-C, 2(r+1))}}{n} = 1 - \frac{0.5 \times \chi^2_{(1-0.90, 2(3+1))}}{69} = 1 - \frac{0.5 \times 13.362}{69} = .9032$$

or 90.32% reliable

9.6 DETERMINING THE APPROPRIATE NUMBER OF LOTS

FDA regulations and guidances, ISO requirements, ICH Q7 guidelines, and other agencies do not prescribe the number of lots necessary to provide objective evidence that a process can consistently produce a result or product meeting its predetermined specifications. However, three production lots has been the traditional industry practice. The manufacturer is expected to have a sound rationale for its choices in determining the number of lots required. The FDA encourages the use of science-based approaches to process validation. The expectation is that the emphasis for demonstrating that validated processes can consistently produce a result or product meeting their predetermined specifications is placed on the manufacturer's process design and development studies.

9.7 CONCLUSION

How to determine the appropriate number of samples necessary for validation purposes is a very complex question. The answer is dependent on many factors, but the most important consideration is patient and user risk driven by product safety and efficacy. When assessing health and safety considerations, one must utilize a risk-based approach in determining a sample size that is adequate and provides a defensible statistical significance. Manufacturers are expected to justify the appropriate number of lots necessary to provide objective evidence that a process can consistently produce a result or product meeting its predetermined specifications.

10

Control Charts for Continuous Process Monitoring

Control charts are an essential tool in satisfying continuous process monitoring requirements for a validated process. *Control charts* are decision-making tools that provide information for timely decisions concerning recently produced products. Control charts are also problem-solving tools that help locate and investigate the causes of poor or marginal quality. The data from control charts can provide useful information when performing revalidation or retrospective validation activities.

Control charts contain a centerline—usually the mathematical average of the samples plotted—upper and lower statistical control limits that define the constraints of common cause variation, and performance data plotted over time.

10.1 CONTROL CHART TYPES AND SELECTION

There are two general classifications of control charts: variables charts and attributes charts (see Table 10.1). *Variables* are things that can be measured: length, temperature, pressure, weight, and so on. *Attributes* are things that are counted: dents, scratches, defects, days, cycles, yes/no decisions, and so on.

10.2 CONTROL CHART INTERPRETATION

A process is said to be *in control* when the control chart does not indicate any out-of-control condition and contains only common causes of variation. If the common cause variation is small, then a control chart can be used to monitor the process. See Figure 10.1 for a representation of stable (in control) and unstable (out of control) processes. If the common cause variation is too large, the process will need to be modified.

When a control chart indicates an out-of-control condition (a point outside the control limits or matching one or more of the criteria below), the assignable causes of variation must be identified and eliminated.

Improper control chart interpretation can lead to several problems, including blaming people for problems they cannot control, spending time and money looking for problems that do not exist, spending time and money on process adjustments or new equipment that are not necessary, taking action where no action is warranted, and asking for worker-related improvements where process or equipment improvements need to be made first.

Table 10.1 Variables and attributes control charts selection.

Variables control charts

Type	Distribution	Sample	Application
$\bar{X}$ and R	Normal	2 ≤ 10	Measurement subgroups
$\bar{X}$ and s	Normal	> 10	Measurement subgroups

Attributes control charts

Type	Distribution	Sample	Application
c	Poisson	Constant	Count number of defects per item
u	Poisson	Varies	Count number of defects per item
np	Binomial	Constant	Count of defective items
p	Binomial	Varies	Count of defective items
g	Binomial	Individual	Interval between rare events

Variables or attributes control charts

Type	Distribution	Sample	Application
X and mR	Normal	1	Individual counts or measurements

Source: M. A. Durivage. 2014. *Practical Engineering, Process, and Reliability Statistics.* Milwaukee: ASQ Quality Press. Used with permission.

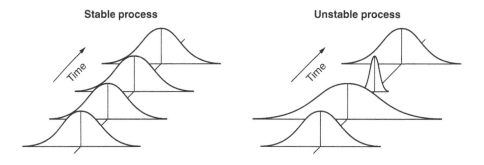

Figure 10.1 Stable and unstable processes.
Source: Adapted from S. A. Wise and D. C. Fair. 1997. *Innovative Control Charting: Practical SPC Solutions for Today's Manufacturing Environment.* Milwaukee: ASQ Quality Press. Used with permission.

The following rules should be used to properly indicate that a process is out of control.

- Rule 1—One point beyond the 3 σ control limit
- Rule 2—Eight or more points on one side of the centerline without crossing
- Rule 3—Four out of five points in zone B or beyond

- Rule 4—Six points or more in a row steadily increasing or decreasing
- Rule 5—Two out of three points in zone A
- Rule 6—14 points in a row alternating up and down
- Rule 7—Any noticeable/predictable pattern, cycle, or trend

Please note that depending on the source, these rules can vary. See Figure 10.2 for control chart interpretation rules.

The target value (which is hopefully the control chart centerline) is closely related to process *accuracy*. The range chart is closely associated with process *precision* (spread or dispersion) (see Figures 10.3 and 10.4).

10.3 $\bar{X}$ AND R CONTROL CHARTS

$\bar{X}$ and R control charts assume a normal distribution and are usually used with a subgroup size of less than 10 (typically 3–5). A minimum of 25 subgroups is necessary to construct the chart.

$\bar{X}$ chart

$$\bar{X} = \frac{\Sigma X}{n} \text{ (Subgroup)}$$

$$\bar{\bar{X}} = \frac{\Sigma \bar{X}}{k} \text{ (Centerline)}$$

$$\bar{X} \text{ UCL} = \bar{\bar{X}} + A_2 * \bar{R}$$

$$\bar{X} \text{ LCL} = \bar{\bar{X}} - A_2 * \bar{R}$$

R chart

$$R = X_n - X_i \text{ (Subgroup)}$$

$$\bar{R} = \frac{\Sigma R}{k} \text{ (Centerline)}$$

$$\bar{R} \text{ UCL} = D_4 * \bar{R}$$

$$\bar{R} \text{ LCL} = D_3 * \bar{R}$$

$$s = \frac{\bar{R}}{d_2} \text{ (Estimate of sigma)}$$

where

n = Subgroup size

k = The number of subgroups

(See Appendix B, Control Chart Constants.)

Example: A process has an $\bar{X}$ of 5.496 and an $\bar{R}$ of 0.065. Twenty-five subgroups of three samples are taken (Table 10.2). Calculate the centerlines and upper and lower control limits, and construct an $\bar{X}$ and R chart (Figure 10.5).

74 Chapter Ten

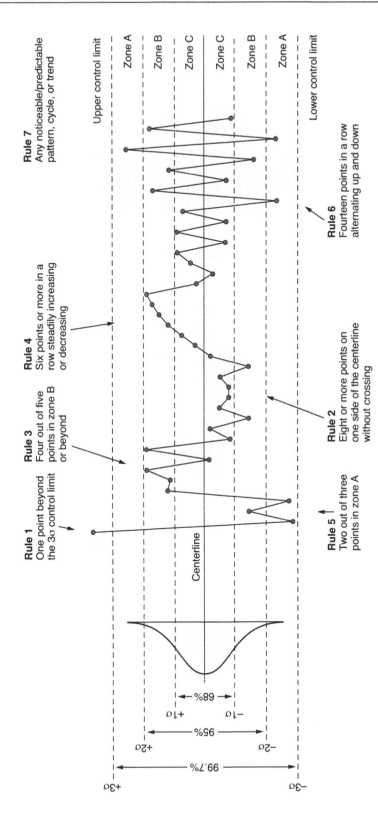

Figure 10.2 Control chart interpretation rules.
Source: Adapted from S. A. Wise and D. C. Fair. 1997. *Innovative Control Charting: Practical SPC Solutions for Today's Manufacturing Environment.* Milwaukee: ASQ Quality Press. Used with permission.

Control Charts for Continuous Process Monitoring   75

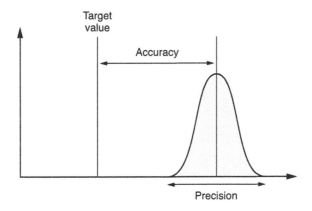

Figure 10.3   Control chart accuracy and precision.
Source: M. A. Durivage. 2014. *Practical Engineering, Process, and Reliability Statistics.* Milwaukee: ASQ Quality Press. Used with permission.

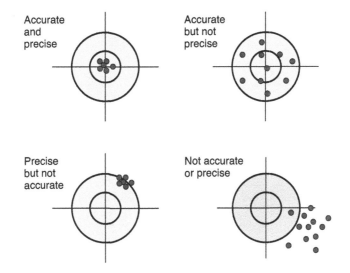

Figure 10.4   Accuracy versus precision.
Source: M. A. Durivage. 2014. *Practical Engineering, Process, and Reliability Statistics.* Milwaukee: ASQ Quality Press. Used with permission.

Table 10.2 Data for $\bar{X}$ and R chart.

Subgroup	$\bar{X}$	R
1	5.447	0.080
2	5.487	0.100
3	5.450	0.060
4	5.450	0.060
5	5.477	0.100
6	5.510	0.020
7	5.510	0.030
8	5.463	0.080
9	5.553	0.040
10	5.510	0.110
11	5.627	0.030
12	5.610	0.110
13	5.507	0.090
14	5.497	0.070
15	5.540	0.080
16	5.413	0.060
17	5.490	0.020
18	5.490	0.060
19	5.467	0.060
20	5.467	0.060
21	5.500	0.070
22	5.477	0.070
23	5.490	0.030
24	5.470	0.080
25	5.490	0.050
Sum	137.390	1.620
Average	5.496	0.065

$$\bar{\bar{X}} = \frac{\Sigma \bar{X}}{k} = \frac{137.390}{25} = 5.496$$

$$\bar{R} = \frac{\Sigma R}{k} = \frac{1.620}{25} = 0.065$$

Control Charts for Continuous Process Monitoring   77

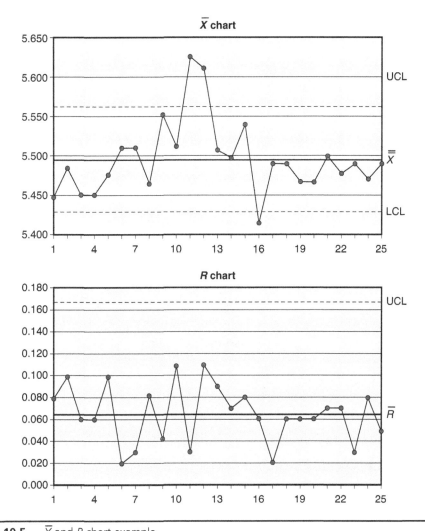

Figure 10.5 $\bar{X}$ and R chart example.
Source: M. A. Durivage. 2014. *Practical Engineering, Process, and Reliability Statistics.* Milwaukee: ASQ Quality Press. Used with permission.

$$\bar{X} \text{ UCL} = \bar{\bar{X}} + A_2 * \bar{R} = 5.496 + 1.023 * 0.065 = 5.535$$

$$\bar{X} \text{ UCL} = \bar{\bar{X}} + A_2 * \bar{R} = 5.496 - 1.023 * 0.065 = 5.430$$

$$\bar{R} \text{ UCL} = D_4 * \bar{R} = 2.574 * 0.065 = .167$$

$$\bar{R} \text{ LCL} = D_3 * \bar{R} = 0 * 0.065 = 0$$

10.4 $\bar{X}$ AND s CONTROL CHARTS

The $\bar{X}$ and s control charts assume a normal distribution and are usually used with a subgroup size of greater than 10. A minimum of 25 subgroups is necessary to construct the chart.

$\bar{X}$ chart	s chart
$\bar{X} = \dfrac{\Sigma X}{n}$ (Subgroup)	$s = \sqrt{\dfrac{\Sigma(X - \bar{X})^2}{n-1}}$ (Subgroup)
$\bar{\bar{X}} = \dfrac{\Sigma \bar{X}}{k}$ (Centerline)	$\bar{s} = \dfrac{\Sigma s}{k}$ (Centerline)
$\bar{X}\ \text{UCL} = \bar{\bar{X}} + A_3 * \bar{s}$	$\bar{s}\ \text{UCL} = B_4 * \bar{s}$
$\bar{X}\ \text{LCL} = \bar{\bar{X}} - A_3 * \bar{s}$	$\bar{s}\ \text{LCL} = B_3 * \bar{s}$

$$s = \dfrac{\bar{s}}{c_4} \quad \text{(Estimate of sigma)}$$

where

n = Subgroup size

k = The number of subgroups

(See Appendix B, Control Chart Constants.)

Example: A process has an $\bar{X}$ of 5.498 and an $\bar{s}$ of 0.046. Twenty-five subgroups of 11 samples are taken (Table 10.3). Calculate the centerlines and the upper and lower control limits, and construct and $\bar{X}$ and s chart (Figure 10.6).

$$\bar{\bar{X}} = \dfrac{\Sigma \bar{X}}{k} = \dfrac{137.488}{25} = 5.498$$

$$\bar{s} = \dfrac{\Sigma s}{k} = \dfrac{1.155}{25} = 0.046$$

$$\bar{X}\ \text{UCL} = \bar{\bar{X}} + A_3 * \bar{s} = 5.498 + 0.927 * 0.046 = 5.541$$

$$\bar{X}\ \text{LCL} = \bar{\bar{X}} - A_3 * \bar{s} = 5.498 - 0.927 * 0.046 = 5.455$$

$$\bar{s}\ \text{UCL} = B_4 * \bar{s} = 1.679 * 0.046 = 0.077$$

$$\bar{s}\ \text{LCL} = B_3 * \bar{s} = 0.321 * 0.046 = 0.015$$

Table 10.3 Data for $\bar{X}$ and s chart.

Subgroup	$\bar{X}$	s
1	5.449	0.032
2	5.487	0.039
3	5.456	0.037
4	5.612	0.121
5	5.479	0.033
6	5.535	0.106
7	5.516	0.016
8	5.465	0.045
9	5.551	0.036
10	5.520	0.031
11	5.489	0.030
12	5.474	0.026
13	5.481	0.035
14	5.480	0.031
15	5.537	0.030
16	5.439	0.047
17	5.505	0.098
18	5.485	0.080
19	5.475	0.071
20	5.590	0.057
21	5.487	0.040
22	5.489	0.039
23	5.492	0.021
24	5.475	0.025
25	5.479	0.029
Sum	**137.448**	**1.155**
Average	**5.498**	**0.046**

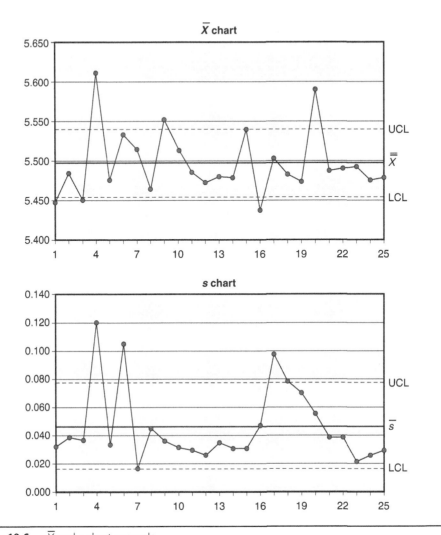

Figure 10.6 $\bar{X}$ and s chart example.
Source: M. A. Durivage. 2014. *Practical Engineering, Process, and Reliability Statistics.* Milwaukee: ASQ Quality Press. Used with permission.

10.5 c-CHARTS

c-charts assume a Poisson distribution and are usually used with a constant sample size, counting the number of defects per item. A minimum of 25 subgroups is necessary to construct the chart.

$$c = \text{(Subgroup count)}$$

$$\bar{c} = \frac{\Sigma c}{k} \text{ (Centerline)}$$

$$\text{UCL} = \bar{c} + 3 * \sqrt{\bar{c}}$$

$$\text{LCL} = \bar{c} - 3 * \sqrt{\bar{c}}$$

(A calculated LCL of less than zero reverts to zero.)

where

k = The number of subgroups

Example: A process is evaluated using a constant sample size of 48 items. When the items are inspected, a count of the number of defects is recorded (Table 10.4). Twenty-five subgroups of 48 samples are taken. Calculate the centerline and the upper and lower control limits, and construct a c-chart (Figure 10.7).

$$\bar{c} = \frac{\Sigma c}{k} = \frac{136}{25} = 5.440$$

$$\text{UCL} = \bar{c} + 3 * \sqrt{\bar{c}} = 5.440 + 3 * \sqrt{5.440} = 12.437$$

$$\text{LCL} = \bar{c} - 3 * \sqrt{\bar{c}} = 5.440 - 3 * \sqrt{5.440} = -1.557 \text{ reverts to } 0$$

Table 10.4 Data for c-chart.

Subgroup	c
1	6
2	7
3	5
4	2
5	11
6	7
7	7
8	0
9	1
10	4
11	15
12	5
13	0
14	6
15	3
16	7
17	6
18	8
19	1
20	7
21	1
22	7
23	11
24	3
25	6
Sum	**136**
Average	**5.440**

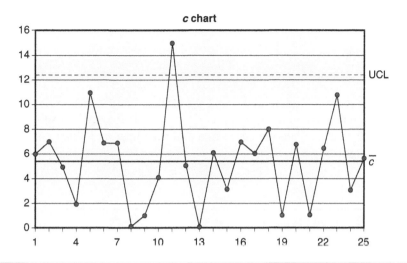

Figure 10.7 c-chart example.
Source: M. A. Durivage. 2014. *Practical Engineering, Process, and Reliability Statistics.* Milwaukee: ASQ Quality Press. Used with permission.

10.6 u-CHARTS

u-charts assume a Poisson distribution and are usually used with a variable sample size (although a constant sample size may be used), counting the number of defects per item. A minimum of 25 subgroups is necessary to construct the chart.

$$u = \frac{c}{n} \text{ (Subgroup)}$$

$$\bar{u} = \frac{\Sigma c}{\Sigma n} \text{ (Centerline)}$$

(Floating control limits) (Static control limits)

$$\text{UCL} = \bar{u} + 3 * \sqrt{\frac{\bar{u}}{n}} \qquad \text{UCL} = \bar{u} + 3 * \sqrt{\frac{\bar{u}}{\Sigma n / k}}$$

$$\text{LCL} = \bar{u} - 3 * \sqrt{\frac{\bar{u}}{n}} \qquad \text{LCL} = \bar{u} - 3 * \sqrt{\frac{\bar{u}}{\Sigma n / k}}$$

(A calculated LCL of less than zero reverts to zero.)

$$s \cong \sqrt{\frac{\bar{u}}{n}} \qquad s \cong \sqrt{\frac{\bar{u}}{\Sigma n / k}}$$

(Estimate of sigma for subgroup) (Estimate of sigma for chart) where

n = Subgroup size

k = The number of subgroups

Example: A process is evaluated using a variable sample size. When the items are inspected, a count of the number of defects is recorded. Twenty-five subgroups are evaluated (Table 10.5). Calculate the centerline and the upper and lower control limits, and construct a u-chart (Figure 10.8).

Table 10.5 Data for u-chart.

Subgroup	n	c	u	UCL	LCL
1	113	77	0.681	1.232	−1.977
2	85	72	0.847	1.274	−1.118
3	99	125	1.263	1.251	−0.737
4	118	121	1.025	1.226	−0.511
5	111	80	0.721	1.235	−0.356
6	59	79	1.339	1.338	−0.241
7	123	117	0.951	1.221	−0.153
8	101	80	0.792	1.248	−0.081
9	105	128	1.219	1.243	−0.022
10	118	111	0.941	1.226	0.029
11	91	66	0.725	1.264	0.072
12	74	103	1.392	1.297	0.109
13	98	99	1.010	1.253	0.143
14	106	110	1.038	1.241	0.172
15	116	75	0.647	1.229	0.199
16	88	123	1.398	1.269	0.223
17	104	43	0.413	1.244	0.245
18	45	77	1.711	1.394	0.265
19	100	91	0.910	1.250	0.283
20	95	114	1.200	1.257	0.300
21	103	102	0.990	1.245	0.316
22	118	76	0.644	1.226	0.331
23	102	71	0.696	1.247	0.345
24	60	90	1.500	1.335	0.357
25	92	88	0.957	1.262	0.370
Sum	2424	2318			

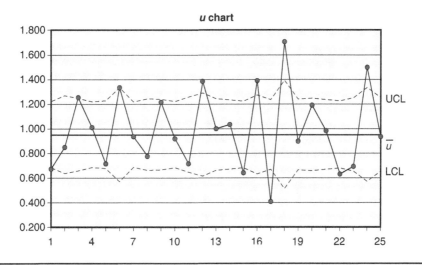

Figure 10.8 *u*-chart example.
Source: M. A. Durivage. 2014. *Practical Engineering, Process, and Reliability Statistics.* Milwaukee: ASQ Quality Press. Used with permission.

$$\bar{u} = \frac{\Sigma c}{\Sigma n} = \frac{2318}{2424} = 0.956$$

$$\text{UCL} = \bar{u} + 3 * \sqrt{\frac{\bar{u}}{n}}$$

$$\text{LCL} = \bar{u} - 3 * \sqrt{\frac{\bar{u}}{n}}$$

The control limits will vary for each subgroup because the sample size *n* varies from group to group.

10.7 np-CHARTS

np-charts assume a binomial distribution and are usually used with a constant sample size, counting the defective items. A minimum of 25 subgroups is necessary to construct the chart.

$$np = \text{(Subgroup count)}$$

$$\overline{np} = \frac{\Sigma np}{k} \quad \text{(Centerline)}$$

$$\text{UCL} = \overline{np} + 3*\sqrt{\overline{np}(1-(\Sigma np / \Sigma n))}$$

$$\text{LCL} = \overline{np} - 3*\sqrt{\overline{np}(1-(\Sigma np / \Sigma n))}$$

(A calculated LCL of less than zero reverts to zero.)

$$s \cong \sqrt{\overline{np}(1-(\Sigma np / \Sigma n))} \quad \text{(Estimate of sigma)}$$

where

n = Subgroup size

k = The number of subgroups

Example: A process is evaluated using a constant sample size of 200 items. When the items are inspected, a count of the number of defective items is recorded. Twenty-five subgroups of 200 samples are taken (Table 10.6). Calculate the centerline and the upper and lower control limits, and construct an np-chart (Figure 10.9).

$$\overline{np} = \frac{\Sigma np}{k} = \frac{100}{25} = 4.000$$

$$\text{UCL} = \overline{np} + 3*\sqrt{\overline{np}(1-(\Sigma np / \Sigma n))} = 4.000 + 3*\sqrt{4.000(1-(100/5000))} = 9.940$$

$$\text{LCL} = \overline{np} - 3*\sqrt{\overline{np}(1-(\Sigma np / \Sigma n))} = 4.000 - 3*\sqrt{4.000(1-(100/5000))} = -1.940,$$

which reverts to zero.

Table 10.6 Data for *np*-chart.

Subgroup	n	np
1	200	2
2	200	5
3	200	3
4	200	5
5	200	11
6	200	1
7	200	5
8	200	6
9	200	2
10	200	0
11	200	5
12	200	8
13	200	4
14	200	2
15	200	6
16	200	3
17	200	4
18	200	6
19	200	4
20	200	1
21	200	1
22	200	2
23	200	5
24	200	0
25	200	9
Sum	**5000**	**100**

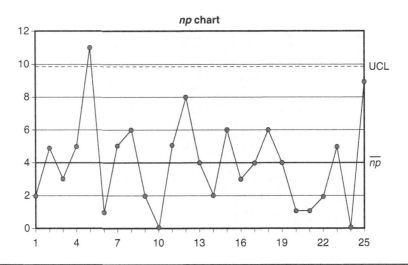

Figure 11.9 *np*-chart example.
Source: M. A. Durivage. 2014. *Practical Engineering, Process, and Reliability Statistics.* Milwaukee: ASQ Quality Press. Used with permission.

10.8 *p*-CHARTS

p-charts assume a binomial distribution and are usually used with a variable sample size (although a constant sample size may be used), counting the defective items. A minimum of 25 subgroups is necessary to construct the chart.

$$p = \frac{np}{n} \quad \text{(Subgroup)}$$

$$\bar{p} = \frac{\Sigma np}{\Sigma n} \quad \text{(Centerline)}$$

(Floating control limits) \qquad (Static control limits)

$$\text{UCL} = \bar{p} + 3 * \sqrt{\bar{p}(1-\bar{p})/n} \qquad \text{UCL} = \bar{p} + 3 * \sqrt{\bar{p}(1-\bar{p})/(\Sigma n / k)}$$

$$\text{LCL} = \bar{p} - 3 * \sqrt{\bar{p}(1-\bar{p})/n} \qquad \text{LCL} = \bar{p} - 3 * \sqrt{\bar{p}(1-\bar{p})/(\Sigma n / k)}$$

(A calculated LCL of less than zero reverts to zero.)

$$s \cong \sqrt{\bar{p}(1-\bar{p})/n} \qquad s \cong \sqrt{\bar{p}(1-\bar{p})/(\Sigma n / k)}$$

(Estimate of sigma for subgroup) \qquad (Estimate of sigma for chart)

Control Charts for Continuous Process Monitoring   89

where

n = Subgroup size

k = The number of subgroups

Example: A process is evaluated using a variable sample size. When the items are inspected, a count of the number of defective items is recorded. Twenty-five subgroups are evaluated (Table 10.7). Calculate the centerline and the upper and lower control limits, and construct a p-chart (Figure 10.10).

Table 10.7   Data for p-chart.

Subgroup	n	np	p	UCL	LCL
1	2108	254	0.120		
2	1175	117	0.100	0.142	0.203
3	1658	248	0.150	0.138	0.175
4	2173	239	0.110	0.135	0.176
5	1720	238	0.138	0.138	0.176
6	1891	250	0.132	0.136	0.175
7	1664	145	0.087	0.138	0.194
8	1685	127	0.075	0.138	0.199
9	1967	327	0.166	0.136	0.167
10	976	95	0.097	0.145	0.212
11	2012	201	0.100	0.136	0.182
12	1187	124	0.104	0.142	0.200
13	1784	173	0.097	0.137	0.187
14	1390	132	0.095	0.140	0.198
15	2075	229	0.110	0.135	0.178
16	2077	236	0.114	0.135	0.177
17	1232	126	0.102	0.142	0.200
18	1914	228	0.119	0.136	0.178
19	2401	315	0.131	0.134	0.168
20	1975	255	0.129	0.136	0.174
21	1365	132	0.097	0.140	0.198
22	1505	117	0.078	0.139	0.203
23	1725	129	0.075	0.137	0.199
24	2105	315	0.150	0.135	0.168
25	1855	242	0.130	0.137	0.176
Sum	43619	4994			

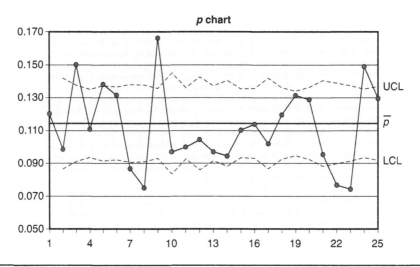

Figure 10.10 p-chart example.
Source: M. A. Durivage. 2014. *Practical Engineering, Process, and Reliability Statistics*. Milwaukee: ASQ Quality Press. Used with permission.

$$\bar{p} = \frac{\Sigma np}{\Sigma n} = \frac{4994}{43619} = 0.114$$

$$\text{UCL} = \bar{p} + 3 * \sqrt{\bar{p}(1-\bar{p})/n}$$

$$\text{LCL} = \bar{p} - 3 * \sqrt{\bar{p}(1-\bar{p})/n}$$

The control limits will vary for each subgroup because the sample size n varies from group to group.

10.9 X AND mR (MOVING RANGE) CONTROL CHARTS

X and mR (moving range) control charts assume a normal distribution and are used with individual values. A minimum of 25 observations is necessary to construct the chart.

X chart

X (Individual observation)

$\bar{X} = \dfrac{\Sigma X}{k}$ (Centerline)

$UCL = \bar{X} + d_2 * \overline{mR}$

$LCL = \bar{X} - d_2 * \overline{mR}$

mR chart

$mR = |X_2 - X_1|, |X_3 - X_2| \ldots$

$\overline{mR} = \dfrac{\Sigma mR}{k-1}$ (Centerline)

$UCL = D_4 * \overline{mR}$

$LCL = 0$

$s = \dfrac{\overline{mR}}{d_2}$ (Estimate of sigma)

where

k = The number of subgroups

(See Appendix B, Control Chart Constants.)

Example: A manager wants to evaluate a low-volume production process. Due to the cost of testing, one sample is measured per shift (Table 10.8). Calculate the centerline and the upper and lower control limits, and construct an X and mR chart (Figure 10.11).

$$\bar{X} = \dfrac{\Sigma X}{k} = \dfrac{174.700}{25} = 6.988$$

$$\overline{mR} = \dfrac{\Sigma mR}{k-1} = \dfrac{7.200}{25-1} = 0.300$$

$$UCL = \bar{X} + d_2 * \overline{mR} = 6.988 + 1.128 * 0.300 = 7.326$$

$$LCL = \bar{X} - d_2 * \overline{mR} = 6.988 - 1.128 * 0.300 = 6.650$$

$$UCL = D_4 * \overline{mR} = 3.267 * 0.300 = 0.980$$

$$LCL = 0$$

Table 10.8 Data for $\bar{X}$ and mR chart.

Subgroup	X	mR
1	7.2	0.000
2	7.5	0.300
3	7.1	0.400
4	6.9	0.200
5	6.8	0.100
6	6.6	0.200
7	6.3	0.300
8	6.9	0.600
9	7.2	0.300
10	7.1	0.100
11	6.9	0.200
12	7.2	0.300
13	7.4	0.200
14	7.5	0.100
15	7.4	0.100
16	7.3	0.100
17	7.7	0.400
18	6.7	1.000
19	7.2	0.500
20	6.8	0.400
21	6.6	0.200
22	6.7	0.100
23	6.2	0.500
24	6.7	0.500
25	6.8	0.100
Sum	**174.700**	**7.200**

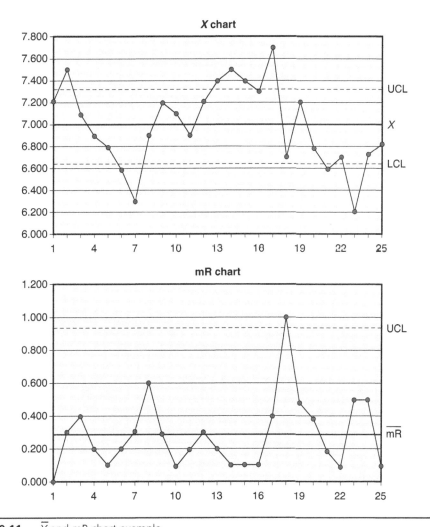

Figure 10.11 $\bar{X}$ and mR chart example.
Source: M. A. Durivage. 2014. *Practical Engineering, Process, and Reliability Statistics.* Milwaukee: ASQ Quality Press. Used with permission.

10.10 CONCLUSION

Control charts are an essential tool in satisfying continuous process monitoring requirements for a validated process. The data from control charts can provide useful information when performing revalidation or retrospective validation activities.

11
Outliers

utliers are data points that do not appear to "belong" to a given set of data. Outlier detection and analysis are extremely important when performing validation work. Without proper identification and analysis, outliers have the potential to negate the results of a validation, resulting in (a) the need to repeat the validation, or (b) development of an incorrect conclusion resulting in an increase in production and product risk.

According to Iglewicz and Hoaglin (1993), outliers can be caused by (a) recording and measurement errors, (b) an incorrect distribution assumption, (c) unknown data structure, or (d) novel phenomenon. Additionally, outliers can be created as a result of a shift in the statistical mean or a change in the variation. There are several tools both visual (for example, histogram, box plot) and analytical that can be employed to determine whether a suspect point is truly an outlier and remove it from consideration when analyzing a data set.

Once an observation is identified as a potential outlier (by means of a graphical or visual inspection), root cause analysis should begin to determine whether an assignable cause can be found for the spurious result (Walfish 2006).

11.1 OUTLIER DETECTION BASED ON THE INTERQUARTILE RANGE

Another method for detecting an outlier when the underlying distribution is unknown and assumed to be nonnormal is the *interquartile range method*. If a suspected point is at least 1.5 interquartile ranges below the first quartile ($Q1$) or at least 1.5 interquartile ranges above the third quartile ($Q3$), the point may be considered an outlier:

$$\text{LPO} = Q1 - 1.5(Q3 - Q1) \text{ and } \text{UPO} = Q3 + 1.5(Q3 - Q1)$$

where

LPO = Lower potential outlier

UPO = Upper potential outlier

$Q1$ = Median value in the first half of the data set

$Q3$ = Median value in the second half of the data set

Example: Given the following data set (please note that the data points should be ordered from smallest value to largest value), calculate the lower and upper outlier limits and determine which points, if any, may be considered an outlier:

$$1, 5, \mathbf{6}, 7, 8, 9, 10, \mathbf{11}, 12, 19$$

$X_{0.25} = 6$ (median value of the first half of the data set)

$X_{0.75} = 11$ (median value of the second half of the data set)

$$\text{LPO} = Q1 - 1.5(Q3 - Q1) = 6 - 1.5(11 - 6) = -1.5$$

and

$$\text{UPO} = Q3 + 1.5(Q3 - Q1) = 11 + 1.5(11 - 6) = 18.5$$

We can reasonably conclude that any point ≤ -1.5 and ≥ 18.5 may be considered an outlier. From the data set, the data point 19 is considered to be an outlier.

11.2 DIXON'S Q TEST

Dixon's Q test is a method that compares the gap (data point in question to the next closest value) divided by the range to determine whether the suspect point is an outlier. It is recommended to use this method only once on a particular set of data. Once the Q value has been calculated, it must be compared to the critical value from Table 11.1. If Q calculated > Q critical, the data point may be considered an outlier with the chosen confidence:

$$Q_{\text{Calc}} = \frac{\text{Gap}}{\text{Range}}$$

Example: Given the following data set (please note that the data points should be ordered from smallest value to largest value), we suspect that the value of 17 may be an outlier. Calculate the Q statistic to determine whether the point may be considered an outlier at the 95% confidence level:

$$1, 3, 6, 7, 8, 9, 10, 11, 12, 23$$

$$Q_{\text{Calc}} = \frac{\text{Gap}}{\text{Range}} = \frac{23 - 12}{23 - 1} = 0.500 \quad (Q_{\text{Crit } \alpha = 0.05} \text{ table value is } 0.466)$$

Since $Q_{\text{Calc}}\, 0.500 > Q_{\text{Crit}}\, 0.466$, we are 95% sure the point is an outlier.

Table 11.1 Selected critical Q values.

n	Q critical 90%	Q critical 95%	Q critical 99%
3	0.941	0.970	0.994
4	0.765	0.829	0.926
5	0.642	0.710	0.821
6	0.560	0.625	0.740
7	0.507	0.568	0.680
8	0.468	0.526	0.634
9	0.437	0.493	0.598
10	0.412	0.466	0.568

11.3 DEAN AND DIXON OUTLIER TEST

The *Dean and Dixon outlier test* is a valid method for detecting outliers when the data are normally distributed. To use this test, the data must be ordered from smallest value to largest value. The formulas are dependent on the sample size:

N	Smallest value test	Largest value test
3 to 7	$r_{10} = \dfrac{X_2 - X_1}{X_n - X_1}$	$r_{10} = \dfrac{X_n - X_{n-1}}{X_n - X_1}$
8 to 10	$r_{11} = \dfrac{X_2 - X_1}{X_{n-1} - X_1}$	$r_{11} = \dfrac{X_n - X_{n-1}}{X_n - X_2}$
11 to 13	$r_{21} = \dfrac{X_3 - X_1}{X_{n-1} - X_1}$	$r_{21} = \dfrac{X_n - X_{n-2}}{X_n - X_2}$
14 to 30	$r_{22} = \dfrac{X_3 - X_1}{X_{n-2} - X_1}$	$r_{22} = \dfrac{X_n - X_{n-2}}{X_n - X_3}$

where

n = Number of data points

(See Appendix C, Critical Values of the Dean and Dixon Outlier Test.)

Example: Given the following data points, verify whether the smallest and largest values are outliers at 95% confidence:

1, 3, 6, 7, 8, 9, 10, 11, 12, 23

Since there are 10 data points ($n = 10$) we must use the second set of equations for 8 to 10 to detect the presence of an outlier.

To detect whether the smallest value is an outlier:

$$r_{11} = \frac{X_2 - X_1}{X_{n-1} - X_1} = \frac{3-1}{12-1} = 0.182 \quad (r_{11\,\alpha=0.05} \text{ table value is } 0.477)$$

Since r_{11} calc is $< r_{11}$ crit, we can conclude that the smallest value is not an outlier at the 95% confidence level.

To detect whether the largest value is an outlier:

$$r_{11} = \frac{X_n - X_{n-1}}{X_n - X_2} = \frac{23-12}{23-3} = 0.550 \quad (r_{11\,\alpha=0.05} \text{ table value is } 0.477)$$

Since r_{11} calc is $> r_{11}$ crit we can conclude that the largest value is an outlier at the 95% confidence level.

11.4 GRUBBS OUTLIER TEST

The *Grubbs outlier test* computes the outlying data point using the average and standard deviation and then compares the calculated value against a critical table value. When a data point is deemed an outlier and removed from the data set, and an additional outlier is suspected, the average and standard deviation must be recalculated.

We calculate the g statistic using

$$g_{\text{Min}} = \frac{\bar{X} - x_{\text{Min}}}{s} \quad \text{or} \quad g_{\text{Max}} = \frac{x_{\text{Max}} - \bar{X}}{s}$$

where

$\bar{X}$ = Average

s = Standard deviation

x_{Min} = Suspected minimum value

x_{Max} = Suspected maximum value

(See Appendix D, Critical Values for the Grubbs Outlier Test.)

Example: Given the following data points, verify whether the smallest and largest values are outliers at 95% confidence:

$$1, 3, 6, 7, 8, 9, 10, 11, 12, 23 \; (\bar{X} = 9, s = 6, \text{ and } n = 10)$$

$$g_{\text{Min}} = \frac{\bar{X} - x_{\text{Min}}}{s} = \frac{9-1}{6} = 1.333 \quad (g_{\text{Crit}\,\alpha=0.05} \text{ table value is } 2.176)$$

Since g_{Min} calc is $< g_{Crit}$, we can conclude that the smallest value is not an outlier at the 95% confidence level.

$$g_{\text{Max}} = \frac{x_{\text{Max}} - \bar{X}}{s} = \frac{23-9}{6} = 2.333 \; (g_{\text{Crit } \alpha=0.05} \text{ table value is } 2.176)$$

Since g_{Max} calc is $> g_{Crit}$, we can conclude that the largest value is an outlier at the 95% confidence level.

11.5 WALSH'S OUTLIER TEST

Walsh's outlier test is a nonparametric test that can be used to detect multiple outliers when the data are not normally distributed. This test requires a minimum sample size of 60. When the sample size (n) is between 60 and 219, the α level of significance is 0.10. When the sample size (n) is 220 or larger, the α level of significance is 0.05. To begin the process, the data must be ordered from smallest to largest. This test requires several calculations and is somewhat cumbersome:

$$c = \sqrt{2n}$$

$$k = r + c$$

$$b^2 = \frac{1}{\alpha}$$

$$a = \frac{1 + b\sqrt{(c-b^2)/(c-1)}}{c - b^2 - 1}$$

Where r smallest points are outliers:

$$X_{(r)} - (1+a)X_{(r+1)} + aX_{(k)} < 0$$

Where r largest points are outliers:

$$X_{(n+1-r)} - (1+a)X_{(n-r)} + aX_{(n+1-k)} > 0$$

Example: 250 parts were measured. It is suspected that the two smallest and the two largest parts are potential outliers. Because $n > 220$, it is appropriate to use an α significance level of 0.05:

$$c = \sqrt{2n} = \sqrt{2*250} = 22.361$$

$$k = r + c = 2 + 22.361 = 24.361$$

$$b^2 = \frac{1}{\alpha} = \frac{1}{.05} = 20$$

$$a = \frac{1+b\sqrt{(c-b^2)/(c-1)}}{c-b^2-1} = \frac{1+4.472\sqrt{(22.361-20)/(22.361-1)}}{22.361-20-1} = 1.829$$

$$a = 1.829 \text{ rounded up} = 2.0$$

Where *r* smallest points are outliers:

$X_2 = 7$

$X_3 = 10$ (values from the data set ordered)

$X_{23} = 42$

$$X_{(r)} - (1+a)X_{(r+1)} + aX_{(k)} < 0 = 7_2 - (1+2)10_3 + 2*42_{23} < 0$$

$$25 < 0$$

Since 25 is not less than 0, we are 95% confident that the two smallest values are outliers. Where *r* largest points are outliers:

$X_{499} = 214$

$X_{498} = 210$ (values from the data set ordered)

$X_{226} = 75$

$$X_{(n+1-r)} - (1+a)X_{(n-r)} + aX_{(n+1-k)} > 0 = 214_{499} - (1+2)210_{498} + 275_{226} > 0$$

$$-141 > 0$$

Since −141 is less than 0, we are 95% confident that the three largest values are not outliers.

11.6 HAMPEL'S METHOD FOR OUTLIER DETECTION

Because the mean and standard deviation are adversely influenced by the presence of outliers, Hampel's method is presented (Hampel 1971; Hampel 1974). For example, the mean will be offset toward the outlier, and the standard deviation will be inflated, leading to errant statistical decisions. Hampel's method is somewhat resistant to these issues as the calculations use the median and *median absolute deviation* (MAD) to detect the presence of outliers.

To determine which, if any, values are outliers, calculate the median value ($\tilde{x}$), calculate the $\text{MAD} = |x_i - \tilde{x}|$, and finally calculate the decision value (median MAD * 5.2). Compare the calculated MAD values to the decision value. Any MAD that exceeds the decision value can be considered an outlier:

$$\text{MAD} = |x_i - \tilde{x}|$$

Decision value (median MAD * 5.2)

Example: The following data were recorded from a manufacturing process with an unknown distribution: 1, 5, 6, 7, 8, 9, 10, 11, 12, and 19. Determine whether any of these values can be considered outliers:

$$\tilde{x} = \frac{8+9}{2} = 8.5$$

Value	MAD $|x_i - \tilde{x}|$
1	$|1 - 8.5| = 7.5$
5	$|5 - 8.5| = 3.5$
6	$|6 - 8.5| = 2.5$
7	$|7 - 8.5| = 1.5$
8	$|8 - 8.5| = 0.5$
9	$|9 - 8.5| = 0.5$
10	$|10 - 8.5| = 1.5$
11	$|11 - 8.5| = 2.5$
12	$|12 - 8.5| = 3.5$
19	$|19 - 8.5| = 10.5$

Value	MAD
8	0.5
9	0.5
7	1.5
10	1.5
6	2.5
11	2.5
5	3.5
12	3.5
1	7.5
19	10.5

$$\text{median MAD} = \frac{2.5 + 2.5}{2} = 2.5$$

Decision value (median MAD * 5.2) = 2.5 * 5.2 = 13

Since none of the MAD values exceed the decision value of 13, none of the values are considered outliers.

11.7 CONCLUSION

Outliers are data points that do not appear to "belong" to a given set of data. Outlier detection and analysis are extremely important when performing validation work. Without proper identification and analysis, outliers have the potential to negate the results of a validation, resulting in (a) the need to repeat the validation, or (b) development of an incorrect conclusion resulting in an increase in production and product risk.

12
Process Capability

P*rocess capability* refers to the ability of a process to meet specifications set by the customer or designer. Process capability compares the output of an in-control process to the specification limits by using various capability indices. A capable process is one where almost all the measurements fall inside the specification limits (Figure 12.1). Process capability data is a useful tool for monitoring validated processes.

12.1 PROCESS CAPABILITY FOR VARIABLES DATA

There are three potential process capability indices for variables data: C_r, C_p, and C_{pk}. Additionally, there are three process capability indices for variables data: P_r, P_p, and P_{pk}. The main difference between the "C" and "P" indices is that C_r, C_p, and C_{pk} are used with sample data to determine whether the process is capable of meeting customer specifications (short term), whereas P_r, P_p, and P_{pk} are used with population data to determine whether the process is capable of meeting customer specifications (long term).

These indices compare the process statistical control limits to the product specifications to determine the process capability. Figure 12.2 demonstrates the relationship between statistical control limits and product specifications.

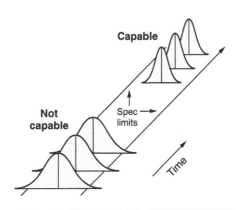

Figure 12.1   Capable process versus not capable process.
Source: Adapted from S. A. Wise and D. C. Fair. 1997. *Innovative Control Charting: Practical SPC Solutions for Today's Manufacturing Environment.* Milwaukee: ASQ Quality Press. Used with permission.

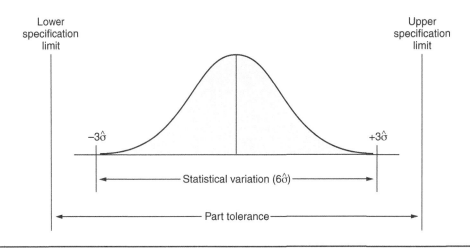

Figure 12.2 Relationship between statistical control limits and product specifications.

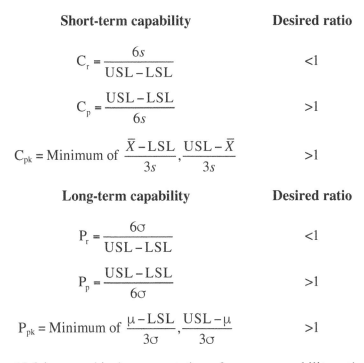

Figure 12.3 is a graphical representation of process capability ratios compared to the statistical control limits and part specification limits.

12.2 PROCESS CAPABILITY FOR ATTRIBUTES DATA

The process capability for attributes data is simply the process average. Ideally, the process average should be zero.

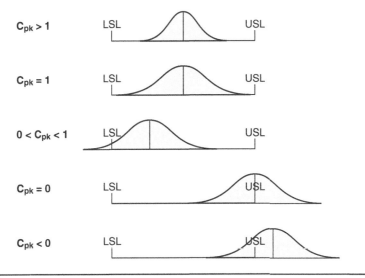

Figure 12.3 Graphical relationship of process capability ratios.

12.3 CONCLUSION

Process capability refers to the ability of a process to meet specifications set by the customer or designer. Process capability compares the output of an in-control process to the specification limits by using various capability indices. A capable process is one where almost all the measurements fall inside the specification limits. Process capability data is a useful tool for monitoring validated processes.

13

Common Validation Issues

Over the years, the authors have seen multiple companies make mistakes while performing process validations. These mistakes have led to regulatory actions as well as financial losses. Hopefully, this book will provide awareness and guidance to help reduce or otherwise eliminate some of these common validation issues. In this chapter, several common mistakes are presented along with potential solutions to address these mistakes. The information presented in this chapter is not to be considered all-inclusive, but is intended to make the reader aware of typical validation pitfalls.

13.1 LINE CLEARANCE NOT PERFORMED

Performing a line clearance prior to and after the execution of a validation is critical to ensure the elimination of comingling of product and packaging as well as minimize the opportunity for contamination and cross-contamination. To prevent this all too common mistake, ensure that the validation protocols call for the performance of a line clearance prior to and after the execution of a validation protocol to prevent mix-ups and the possibility of contamination and cross-contamination.

13.2 DEVIATIONS—OPENING, INVESTIGATION, AND CLOSING

While executing validation protocols, it is quite possible to encounter a deviation. If a deviation does occur, it does not necessarily mean the validation has failed. However, when a deviation occurs, it is important to document the reason for the deviation, investigate the cause(s), and properly close the deviation prior to writing the validation report. All discussions pertaining to the deviation, including written rationale for the acceptance or rejection of a deviation, should be included in the report.

13.3 DISPOSITION OF OQ PRODUCT PRODUCED

Product produced during an operational qualification (OQ) run can be retained as objective evidence or should be destroyed. In any case, product produced during an OQ should not be used for commercial sale. This is especially true when the product being produced is governed by regulatory authorities. It is very important to properly document the disposition of all products produced during the OQ run.

13.4 USING A SIMULANT OR DUNNAGE FOR OQ

Using a simulant or dunnage for OQ is extremely important to ensure that the product itself does not have a deleterious effect on the process being validated. For example, if a packaging validation is being executed, it is imperative that a simulant or dunnage be used to ensure that the product does not adversely affect the process. It is acceptable to use parts that have been scrapped as long as they are properly identified or labeled and are substantially equivalent to the end product being produced.

13.5 BRACKETING STRATEGY/RATIONALE FOR FAMILY OF PARTS

When validating a family of parts, it is not necessary or required that each individual part number be validated. However, a bracketing strategy and appropriate rationale should be documented and included in the protocol. The stategy should specifically explain why the parts selected represent the worst-case scenario. For example, a family of parts includes 10 unique part numbers; the only feature that is different is the length of the part. Validating the shortest and longest parts can potentially demonstrate the ability of the process to produce all of the parts within the family. Therefore, a rationale explaining the bracketing strategy could be that the shortest and longest parts were selected because they represent the worst-case scenario for the family of parts being validated.

13.6 FIRST ARTICLE LAYOUT (FAL)/FIRST ARTICLE INSPECTION (FAI)

Not all features on the product being produced are critical to quality. It is not required that each and every feature or specification be fully validated as long as the risk management documents (FMEA) support the validation decision. However, a first article layout strategy should be utilized to demonstrate the process's ability to consistently produce the non–critical to quality features of the product being produced. Generally, it is acceptable to perform an FAL/FAI on 3–5 parts. This information should be included as an appendix to the validation protocol report.

If a non–critical to quality feature becomes problematic because of customer complaints or other issues, it is best to revalidate the process and include the feature as a critical-to-quality feature and monitor accordingly.

13.7 NOT PRODUCING ENOUGH SAMPLES

Sometimes, while executing a validation protocol, something happens and the required number of samples (in accordance with the protocol) are not available. The actions taken in this situation will depend on the risk associated with the feature. In any event, a deviation should be initiated. It may be best to plan on producing a few additional samples when yield loss is expected, to ensure there are enough samples available to satisfy the requirements of the protocol. Remember, if the protocol requires 60 samples, and 63 samples are produced, the extra samples can be saved as reserve units. Manufacturing more samples than required is a conservative approach and can be easily defended. However, there is no requirement to utilize the additional parts.

13.8 NOT RECORDING THE LOT NUMBERS OF THE MATERIALS USED DURING THE VALIDATION

A mistake commonly made is not recording the lot numbers of the materials used during the validation. It is very important to record the information pertaining to all materials used during the validation for the purposes of identification and traceability, especially if issues with the product arise in the future. It is best practice to use products from different lot numbers and suppliers whenever possible to demonstrate the robustness of the process.

13.9 TRAINING

Properly training the individuals responsible for writing and executing the validation protocol and report is a requirement. Not only should these individuals be trained in the applicable standard operating procedures, industry standards (for example, AAMI, ISO, ASTM) and work instructions, there should be documented evidence of training to the validation protocol.

13.10 ESTABLISHING REVALIDATION/ RETROSPECTIVE VALIDATION CRITERIA AND INTERVALS

Once a validation protocol is executed, completed, and approved, consideration should be given to revalidation/retrospective validation criteria and intervals. As shown in

Chapter 7, there are many cases where revalidation activities should occur. The interval for revalidation/retrospective validation should be documented and based on risk.

13.11 USING UNCALIBRATED INSPECTION, MEASURING, AND TEST EQUIPMENT (IMTE)

Using uncalibrated IMTE is a common problem. All IMTE used to execute a validation protocol shall be current in its calibration status, and the serial number of the equipment employed recorded. The use of IMTE that is not current on calibration can be an audit or inspection nonconformance. The information gathered during the execution protocol will be suspect.

13.12 NOT VERIFYING THE MEASUREMENT SYSTEM

Performing a gage repeatability and reproducibility (GR&R) study, measurement systems analysis (MSA), or test method validation (TMV) is critical to provide a complete and accurate evaluation of the process. If the measurement system is not capable, the information gathered during the execution of the validation protocol will be suspect. It is good practice to reference the appropriate GR&R/MSA/TMV within the validation protocol.

13.13 NOT VALIDATING IDENTICAL MACHINES

It is an accepted concept that two "identical" pieces of equipment may not be 100% identical in their performance parameters. Each machine may exhibit minor, or in some cases major, variations in their performance. Therefore, it is never acceptable to not validate each machine. Experience has lent itself to the decision to have a validation protocol and report for each machine. The primary reason for this rule is that if something changes on one machine, revalidation of the other machines will not be required. Remember, if there are four "identical" machines, write one validation protocol and copy it three times, and just change the machine number.

13.14 NOT VALIDATING IDENTICAL TOOLING

Just as there are no "identical" machines, tooling and molds are not "identical" either. All tools and molds should be validated. This process is generally referred to as *tool qualification*. Machine/tool/mold combinations should be documented to ensure that only the validated combinations are used for production parts.

13.15 APPROVALS

Another common mistake found in validation documents is not having the appropriate approvals on the validation protocols and reports. Validation activities are team activities generally requiring the participation of the manufacturing and quality functions. While there is no requirement as to who must sign and approve these documents other than that the individuals must be "qualified," it is best to procedurally define the appropriate individuals required to approve validation protocols, deviations, and reports.

13.16 CHANGE CONTROL

Validation protocols and reports should be placed into an organization's change control process. Any changes made to the equipment, process, or materials shall be evaluated, documented, and revalidated, if deemed appropriate.

13.17 NOT PLANNING/PERFORMING CONTINUOUS PROCESS MONITORING

Continuous process monitoring is required to ensure that the specified requirements are consistently met. This monitoring is usually done through the use of control charts and review of other data sources (nonconformance reports [NCRs], complaints, product yields, and so on) (see Chapter 10).

13.18 NOT HAVING A VALIDATION MASTER PLAN

A validation master plan, or master validation plan, is used to provide an overview of all validations. Having a documented plan is essentially the road map for an organization's approach to validation. When properly written, the VMP will contain requirements supporting IQ, OQ, PQ, and PPQ (see Chapter 6).

13.19 SAMPLE SIZE NOT JUSTIFIED

A very common problem seen with many validations is the lack of sample size rationale. The use of a risk-based, statistically significant sample size is a fundamental requirement for an acceptable approach to validation. A statistical techniques procedure and/or a sampling plan procedure are usually used to provide consistency, and for the basis of the written rationale needed to justify the sample size used (see Chapter 9).

13.20 THE LACK OF PREDEFINED ACCEPTANCE CRITERIA

Not having predefined acceptance criteria can be a cause of audit or inspection findings. Acceptance criteria need to be clearly defined, unambiguous, and consistently achievable, and meet the intent of the required design and performance specifications. Acceptance criteria can be based on standards, industry norms, or regulatory requirements, or be user defined.

13.21 CONCLUSION

This chapter has provided examples of several common mistakes along with potential solutions to address the errors commonly seen by the authors in validation activities. The information presented in this chapter is not to be considered all-inclusive, but is intended to make the reader aware of typical validation pitfalls.

Appendix A
Distribution of the Chi-Square

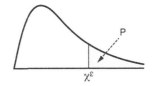

df	0.995	0.99	0.95	0.9	0.1	0.05	0.01	0.005
1	—	—	0.004	0.016	2.706	3.841	6.635	7.879
2	0.010	0.020	0.103	0.211	4.605	5.991	9.210	10.597
3	0.072	0.115	0.352	0.584	6.251	7.815	11.345	12.838
4	0.207	0.297	0.711	1.064	7.779	9.488	13.277	14.860
5	0.412	0.554	1.145	1.610	9.236	11.070	15.086	16.750
6	0.676	0.872	1.635	2.204	10.645	12.592	16.812	18.548
7	0.989	1.239	2.167	2.833	12.017	14.067	18.475	20.278
8	1.344	1.646	2.733	3.490	13.362	15.507	20.090	21.955
9	1.735	2.088	3.325	4.168	14.684	16.919	21.666	23.589
10	2.156	2.558	3.940	4.865	15.987	18.307	23.209	25.188
11	2.603	3.053	4.575	5.578	17.275	19.675	24.725	26.757
12	3.074	3.571	5.226	6.304	18.549	21.026	26.217	28.300
13	3.565	4.107	5.892	7.042	19.812	22.362	27.688	29.819
14	4.075	4.660	6.571	7.790	21.064	23.685	29.141	31.319
15	4.601	5.229	7.261	8.547	22.307	24.996	30.578	32.801
16	5.142	5.812	7.962	9.312	23.542	26.296	32.000	34.267
17	5.697	6.408	8.672	10.085	24.769	27.587	33.409	35.718
18	6.265	7.015	9.390	10.865	25.989	28.869	34.805	37.156
19	6.844	7.633	10.117	11.651	27.204	30.144	36.191	38.582
20	7.434	8.260	10.851	12.443	28.412	31.410	37.566	39.997
21	8.034	8.897	11.591	13.240	29.615	32.671	38.932	41.401
22	8.643	9.542	12.338	14.041	30.813	33.924	40.289	42.796

Continued

Continued

df	0.995	0.99	0.95	0.9	0.1	0.05	0.01	0.005
23	9.260	10.196	13.091	14.848	32.007	35.172	41.638	44.181
24	9.886	10.856	13.848	15.659	33.196	36.415	42.980	45.559
25	10.520	11.524	14.611	16.473	34.382	37.652	44.314	46.928
26	11.160	12.198	15.379	17.292	35.563	38.885	45.642	48.290
27	11.808	12.879	16.151	18.114	36.741	40.113	46.963	49.645
28	12.461	13.565	16.928	18.939	37.916	41.337	48.278	50.993
29	13.121	14.256	17.708	19.768	39.087	42.557	49.588	52.336
30	13.787	14.953	18.493	20.599	40.256	43.773	50.892	53.672
50	27.99	29.71	34.76	37.69	63.167	67.505	76.154	79.49
100	67.328	70.065	77.929	82.358	118.498	124.342	135.807	140.169

Appendix B
Control Chart Constants

(n)	A	A_2	D_1	D_2	D_3	D_4	A_3	B_3	B_4	d_2	d_3	c_4
2	2.121	1.880	0.000	3.686	0.000	3.267	2.659	0.000	3.267	1.128	0.853	0.798
3	1.732	1.023	0.000	4.358	0.000	2.574	1.954	0.000	2.568	1.693	0.888	0.886
4	1.500	0.729	0.000	4.698	0.000	2.282	1.628	0.000	2.266	2.059	0.880	0.921
5	1.342	0.577	0.000	4.918	0.000	2.114	1.427	0.000	2.089	2.326	0.864	0.940
6	1.225	0.483	0.000	5.078	0.000	2.004	1.287	0.030	1.970	2.534	0.848	0.952
7	1.134	0.419	0.204	5.204	0.076	1.924	1.182	0.118	1.882	2.704	0.833	0.959
8	1.061	0.373	0.388	5.306	0.136	1.864	1.099	0.185	1.815	2.847	0.820	0.965
9	1.000	0.337	0.547	5.393	0.184	1.816	1.032	0.239	1.761	2.970	0.808	0.969
10	0.949	0.308	0.687	5.469	0.223	1.777	0.975	0.284	1.716	3.078	0.797	0.973
11	0.905	0.285	0.811	5.535	0.256	1.744	0.927	0.321	1.679	3.173	0.787	0.975
12	0.866	0.266	0.922	5.594	0.283	1.717	0.886	0.354	1.646	3.258	0.778	0.978
13	0.832	0.249	1.025	5.647	0.307	1.693	0.850	0.382	1.618	3.336	0.770	0.979
14	0.802	0.235	1.118	5.696	0.328	1.672	0.817	0.406	1.594	3.407	0.763	0.981
15	0.775	0.223	1.203	5.741	0.347	1.653	0.789	0.428	1.572	3.472	0.756	0.982
16	0.750	0.212	1.282	5.782	0.363	1.637	0.763	0.448	1.552	3.532	0.750	0.984
17	0.728	0.203	1.356	5.820	0.378	1.622	0.739	0.466	1.534	3.588	0.744	0.985
18	0.707	0.194	1.424	5.856	0.391	1.608	0.718	0.482	1.518	3.640	0.739	0.985
19	0.688	0.187	1.487	5.891	0.403	1.597	0.698	0.497	1.503	3.689	0.733	0.986
20	0.671	0.180	1.549	5.921	0.415	1.585	0.680	0.510	1.490	3.735	0.729	0.987
21	0.655	0.173	1.605	5.951	0.425	1.575	0.663	0.523	1.477	3.778	0.724	0.988
22	0.640	0.167	1.659	5.979	0.434	1.566	0.647	0.534	1.466	3.819	0.720	0.988
23	0.626	0.162	1.710	6.006	0.443	1.557	0.633	0.545	1.455	3.858	0.716	0.989
24	0.612	0.157	1.759	6.031	0.451	1.548	0.619	0.555	1.445	3.895	0.712	0.989
25	0.600	0.153	1.806	6.056	0.459	1.541	0.606	0.565	1.435	3.931	0.708	0.990

Appendix C
Critical Values of the Dean and Dixon Outlier Test

	$\alpha = 0.001$	$\alpha = 0.002$	$\alpha = 0.005$	$\alpha = 0.01$	$\alpha = 0.02$	$\alpha = 0.05$	$\alpha = 0.1$	$\alpha = 0.2$
n				r_{10}				
3	0.999	0.998	0.994	0.988	0.976	0.941	0.886	0.782
4	0.964	0.949	0.921	0.889	0.847	0.766	0.679	0.561
5	0.895	0.869	0.824	0.782	0.729	0.643	0.559	0.452
6	0.822	0.792	0.744	0.698	0.646	0.563	0.484	0.387
7	0.763	0.731	0.681	0.636	0.587	0.507	0.433	0.344
n				r_{11}				
8	0.799	0.769	0.724	0.682	0.633	0.554	0.48	0.386
9	0.75	0.72	0.675	0.634	0.586	0.512	0.441	0.352
10	0.713	0.683	0.637	0.597	0.551	0.477	0.409	0.325
n				r_{21}				
11	0.77	0.746	0.708	0.674	0.636	0.575	0.518	0.445
12	0.739	0.714	0.676	0.643	0.605	0.546	0.489	0.42
13	0.713	0.687	0.649	0.617	0.58	0.522	0.467	0.399
n				r_{22}				
14	0.732	0.708	0.672	0.64	0.603	0.546	0.491	0.422
15	0.708	0.685	0.648	0.617	0.582	0.524	0.47	0.403
16	0.691	0.667	0.63	0.598	0.562	0.505	0.453	0.386
17	0.671	0.647	0.611	0.58	0.545	0.489	0.437	0.373
18	0.652	0.628	0.594	0.564	0.529	0.475	0.424	0.361
19	0.64	0.617	0.581	0.551	0.517	0.462	0.412	0.349
20	0.627	0.604	0.568	0.538	0.503	0.45	0.401	0.339
25	0.574	0.55	0.517	0.489	0.457	0.406	0.359	0.302
30	0.539	0.517	0.484	0.456	0.425	0.376	0.332	0.278

Appendix D
Critical Values for the Grubbs Outlier Test

n	α = 0.001	α = 0.005	α = 0.01	α = 0.025	α = 0.05	α = 0.1
3	1.155	1.155	1.155	1.154	1.153	1.148
4	1.499	1.496	1.492	1.481	1.462	1.425
5	1.780	1.764	1.749	1.715	1.671	1.602
6	2.011	1.973	1.944	1.887	1.822	1.729
7	2.201	2.139	2.097	2.020	1.938	1.828
8	2.359	2.274	2.221	2.127	2.032	1.909
9	2.492	2.387	2.323	2.215	2.110	1.977
10	2.606	2.482	2.410	2.290	2.176	2.036
11	2.705	2.564	2.484	2.355	2.234	2.088
12	2.791	2.636	2.549	2.412	2.285	2.134
13	2.867	2.699	2.607	2.462	2.331	2.176
14	2.935	2.755	2.658	2.507	2.372	2.213
15	2.997	2.806	2.705	2.548	2.409	2.248
16	3.052	2.852	2.747	2.586	2.443	2.279
17	3.102	2.894	2.785	2.620	2.475	2.309
18	3.148	2.932	2.821	2.652	2.504	2.336
19	3.191	2.968	2.853	2.681	2.531	2.361
20	3.230	3.001	2.884	2.708	2.557	2.385
22	3.300	3.060	2.939	2.758	2.603	2.429
24	3.362	3.112	2.987	2.802	2.644	2.468
26	3.416	3.158	3.029	2.841	2.681	2.503
28	3.464	3.199	3.068	2.876	2.714	2.536
30	3.507	3.236	3.103	2.908	2.745	2.565
35	3.599	3.316	3.178	2.978	2.812	2.630
40	3.674	3.381	3.239	3.036	2.868	2.684
45	3.736	3.435	3.292	3.085	2.915	2.731
50	3.788	3.482	3.337	3.128	2.957	2.772

Continued

Continued

n	α = 0.001	α = 0.005	α = 0.01	α = 0.025	α = 0.05	α = 0.1
55	3.834	3.524	3.376	3.166	2.994	2.808
60	3.874	3.560	3.411	3.200	3.027	2.841
65	3.910	3.592	3.443	3.230	3.057	2.871
70	3.942	3.622	3.471	3.258	3.084	2.898
75	3.971	3.648	3.497	3.283	3.109	2.923
80	3.997	3.673	3.521	3.306	3.132	2.946
85	4.022	3.695	3.543	3.328	3.153	2.967
90	4.044	3.716	3.563	3.348	3.173	2.987
95	4.065	3.736	3.582	3.366	3.192	3.006
100	4.084	3.754	3.600	3.384	3.210	3.024
110	4.119	3.787	3.633	3.416	3.242	3.056
120	4.150	3.817	3.662	3.445	3.271	3.086
130	4.178	3.843	3.688	3.471	3.297	3.112
140	4.203	3.867	3.712	3.495	3.321	3.136
150	4.225	3.889	3.734	3.517	3.343	3.159
160	4.246	3.910	3.754	3.537	3.363	3.180
170	4.266	3.928	3.773	3.556	3.382	3.199
180	4.284	3.946	3.790	3.574	3.400	3.217
190	4.300	3.962	3.807	3.590	3.417	3.234
200	4.316	3.978	3.822	3.606	3.432	3.250
250	4.381	4.043	3.887	3.671	3.499	3.318
300	4.432	4.094	3.938	3.724	3.552	3.373
350	4.474	4.135	3.981	3.767	3.596	3.418
400	4.508	4.171	4.017	3.803	3.634	3.457
450	4.538	4.201	4.048	3.835	3.666	3.490
500	4.565	4.228	4.075	3.863	3.695	3.520
600	4.609	4.274	4.121	3.911	3.744	3.570
700	4.646	4.312	4.160	3.951	3.785	3.612
800	4.677	4.344	4.193	3.984	3.820	3.648
900	4.704	4.372	4.221	4.014	3.850	3.679
1000	4.728	4.397	4.247	4.040	3.877	3.707
1500	4.817	4.490	4.342	4.138	3.978	3.812
2000	4.878	4.553	4.407	4.206	4.048	3.884

Glossary

acceptance number—The maximum number of defects or defectives allowable in a sampling lot for the lot to be acceptable.

acceptance quality limit (AQL)—In a continuing series of lots, a quality level that, for the purpose of sampling inspection, is the limit of a satisfactory process average.

acceptance sampling—Inspection of a sample from a lot to decide whether to accept that lot. There are two types: attributes sampling and variables sampling. In *attributes* sampling, the presence or absence of a characteristic is noted in each of the units inspected. In *variables* sampling, the numerical magnitude of a characteristic is measured and recorded for each inspected unit; this involves reference to a continuous scale of some kind.

acceptance sampling plan—A specific plan that indicates the sampling sizes and associated acceptance or nonacceptance criteria to be used. In attributes sampling, for example, there are single, double, multiple, sequential, chain, and skip-lot sampling plans. In variables sampling, there are single, double, and sequential sampling plans. For detailed descriptions of these plans, see the standard ANSI/ISO/ASQ A3534-2-1993 *Statistics—Vocabulary and symbols—Statistical quality control*.

accuracy—The closeness of a measured value to a standard or known value.

attributes data—Go/no-go information. The control charts based on attributes data include percent chart, number of affected units chart, count chart, count per unit chart, quality score chart, and demerit chart.

attributes, method of—Method of measuring quality that consists of noting the presence (or absence) of some characteristic (attribute) in each of the units under consideration and counting how many units do (or do not) possess it. Example: Go/no-go gauging of a dimension.

average chart—A control chart in which the subgroup average, $\bar{X}$, is used to evaluate the stability of the process level.

average outgoing quality (AOQ)—The expected average quality level of an outgoing product for a given value of incoming product quality.

average outgoing quality limit (AOQL)—The maximum average outgoing quality over all possible levels of incoming quality for a given acceptance sampling plan and disposal specification.

average run length (ARL)—On a control chart, the number of subgroups expected to be inspected before a shift in magnitude takes place.

average sample number (ASN)—The average number of sample units inspected per lot when reaching decisions to accept or reject.

average total inspection (ATI)—The average number of units inspected per lot, including all units in rejected lots (applicable when the procedure calls for 100% inspection of rejected lots).

batch lot—A definite quantity of some product manufactured under conditions of production that are considered uniform.

calibration—The comparison of a measurement instrument or system of unverified accuracy to a measurement instrument or system of known accuracy to detect any variation from the required performance specification.

capability—The total range of inherent variation in a stable process determined by using data from control charts.

centerline—A line on a graph that represents the overall average (mean) operating level of the process.

central tendency—The tendency of data gathered from a process to cluster toward a middle value somewhere between the high and low values of measurement.

chain sampling plan—In acceptance sampling, a plan in which the criteria for acceptance and rejection apply to the cumulative sampling results for the current lot and one or more immediately preceding lots.

characteristic—The factors, elements, or measures that define and differentiate a process, function, product, service, or other entity.

chart—A tool for organizing, summarizing, and depicting data in graphic form.

classification of defects—The listing of possible defects of a unit, classified according to their seriousness. Commonly used classifications include class A, class B, class C, class D; or critical, major, minor, and incidental; or critical, major and minor. Definitions of these classifications require careful preparation and tailoring to the product(s) being sampled to ensure assignment of a defect to the proper classification. A separate acceptance sampling plan is generally applied to each class of defects.

common causes—Causes of variation that are inherent in a process over time. They affect every outcome of the process and everyone working in the process. See also **special causes**.

complaint tracking—Collecting data, disseminating them to appropriate persons for resolution, monitoring complaint resolution progress, and communicating results.

compliance—The state of an organization that meets prescribed specifications, contract terms, regulations, or standards.

conformance—An affirmative indication or judgment that a product or service has met the requirements of a relevant specification, contract, or regulation.

consumer—The external customer to whom a product or service is ultimately delivered; also called *end user*.

consumer's risk—Pertains to sampling and the potential risk that bad products will be accepted and shipped to the consumer.

continuous sampling plan—In acceptance sampling, a plan, intended for application to a continuous flow of individual units of product, that involves acceptance and rejection on a unit-by-unit basis and employs alternate periods of 100% inspection and sampling. The relative amount of 100% inspection depends on the quality of submitted product. Continuous sampling plans usually require that each t period of 100% inspection be continued until a specified number, i, of consecutively inspected units are found clear of defects. Note: For single-level continuous sampling plans, a single d sampling rate (for example, inspect one unit in five or one unit in 10) is used during sampling. For multilevel continuous sampling plans, two or more sampling rates can be used. The rate at any given time depends on the quality of submitted product.

control chart—A chart with upper and lower control limits on which values of some statistical measure for a series of samples or subgroups are plotted. The chart frequently shows a central line to help detect a trend of plotted values toward either control limit.

control limits—The natural boundaries of a process within specified confidence levels, expressed as the upper control limit (UCL) and the lower control limit (LCL).

control plan (CP)—Written descriptions of the systems for controlling part and process quality by addressing the key characteristics and engineering requirements.

corrective action—A solution meant to reduce or eliminate an identified problem.

corrective action recommendation (CAR)—The full-cycle corrective action tool that offers ease and simplicity of employee involvement in the corrective action/process improvement cycle.

correlation (statistical)—A measure of the relationship between two data sets of variables.

count chart—A control chart for evaluating the stability of a process in terms of the count of events of a given classification occurring in a sample; known as a c-*chart*.

count per unit chart—A control chart for evaluating the stability of a process in terms of the average count of events of a given classification per unit occurring in a sample.

C_p—A comparison of the specification limits divided by six sigma. The greater the C_p value, the better the process capability.

C_{pk} **index**—Equals the lesser of the USL minus the mean divided by three sigma (or the mean) minus the LSL divided by three sigma. The greater the C_{pk} value, the better the process cabability.

critical processes—Processes that present serious potential dangers to human life, health, and the environment or that risk the loss of significant sums of money or customers.

cumulative sum control chart (CUSUM)—A control chart on which the plotted value is the cumulative sum of deviations of successive samples from a target value. The ordinate of each plotted point represents the algebraic sum of the previous ordinate and the most recent deviations from the target.

defect—A product's or service's nonfulfillment of an intended requirement or reasonable expectation for use, including safety considerations. There are four classes of defects: class 1, very serious, leads directly to severe injury or catastrophic economic loss; class 2, serious, leads directly to significant injury or significant economic loss; class 3, major, is related to major problems with respect to intended normal or reasonably foreseeable use; and class 4, minor, is related to minor problems with respect to intended normal or reasonably foreseeable use. See also **nonconformity**.

defective—A defective unit; a unit of product that contains one or more defects with respect to the quality characteristic(s) under consideration.

design of experiments (DOE)—A branch of applied statistics dealing with planning, conducting, analyzing, and interpreting controlled tests to evaluate the factors that control the value of a parameter or group of parameters.

design record—Engineering requirements, typically contained in various formats; examples include engineering drawings, math data, and referenced specifications.

deviation—In numerical data sets, the difference or distance of an individual observation or data value from the center point (often the mean) of the set distribution.

double sampling—Sampling inspection in which the inspection of the first sample leads to a decision to accept a lot, reject it, or take a second sample; the inspection of a second sample, when required, then leads to a decision to accept or to reject the lot.

dunnage—Materials used to simulate production product. Typically, rejected parts are used for validation purposes if the cost of actual parts is cost prohibitive.

experimental design—A formal plan that details the specifics for conducting an experiment, such as which responses, factors, levels, blocks, treatments, and tools are to be used.

failure—The inability of an item, product, or service to perform required functions on demand due to one or more defects.

failure mode analysis (FMA)—A procedure for determining which malfunction symptoms appear immediately before or after a failure of a critical parameter in a system. After all possible causes are listed for each symptom, the product is designed to eliminate the problems.

failure mode and effects analysis (FMEA)—A systematized group of activities for recognizing and evaluating the potential failure of a product or process and its effects, identifying actions that could eliminate or reduce the occurrence of the potential failure, and documenting the process.

first pass yield (FPY)—Also referred to as the *quality rate*, the percentage of units that completes a process and meets quality guidelines without being scrapped, rerun, retested, returned, or diverted into an off-line repair area. FPY is calculated by dividing the units entering the process minus the defective units by the total number of units entering the process.

gage repeatability and reproducibility (GR&R)—The evaluation of a gauging instrument's accuracy by determining whether its measurements are repeatable (there is close agreement between a number of consecutive measurements of the output for the same value of the input under the same operating conditions) and reproducible (there is close agreement between repeated measurements of the output for the same value of input made under the same operating conditions over a period of time).

go/no-go—State of a unit or product. Two parameters are possible: go (conforms to specifications) and no-go (does not conform to specifications).

inspection lot—A collection of similar units or a specific quantity of similar material offered for inspection and acceptance at one time.

installation qualification (IQ)—Establishing by objective evidence that all key aspects of the process equipment and ancillary system installation adhere to the manufacturer's approved specification and that the recommendations of the supplier of the equipment are suitably considered.

key process characteristic—A process parameter that can affect safety or compliance with regulations, fit, function, performance, or subsequent processing of product.

key product characteristic—A product characteristic that can affect safety or compliance with regulations, fit, function, performance, or subsequent processing of product.

layout inspection—The complete measurement of all dimensions shown on a design record.

lot—A defined quantity of product accumulated under conditions considered uniform for sampling purposes.

lot quality—The value of percentage defective or of defects per hundred units in a lot.

lot size (also referred to as *N*)—The number of units in a lot.

lot tolerance percentage defective (LTPD)—Expressed in percentage defective, the poorest quality in an individual lot that should be accepted. Note: LTPD is used as a basis for some inspection systems and is commonly associated with a small consumer risk.

lower control limit (LCL)—Control limit for points below the central line in a control chart.

measure—The criteria, metric, or means to which a comparison is made with output.

measurement—The act or process of quantitatively comparing results with requirements.

measurement system—All operations, procedures, devices, and other equipment or personnel used to assign a value to the characteristic being measured.

measurement uncertainty—The result of random effects and imperfect correction of systemic effects in obtaining a measurement value that results in variation from the actual true value; also known as *measurement error*.

metrology—The science of weights and measures or of measurement; a system of weights and measures.

multiple sampling—Sampling inspection in which, after each sample is inspected, the decision is made to accept a lot, reject it, or take another sample. But there is a prescribed maximum number of samples after which a decision to accept or reject the lot must be reached. Note: Multiple sampling as defined here has sometimes been called "sequential *n* sampling" or "truncated sequential *e* sampling." The term *multiple sampling* is recommended.

multivariate control chart—A control chart for evaluating the stability of a process in terms of the levels of two or more variables or characteristics.

n—The number of units in a sample.

N—The number of units in a population.

nonconforming record (NCR)—A permanent record—made in writing—for accounting and preserving the knowledge of a nonconforming condition for the purpose of documenting facts or events.

nonconformity—The nonfulfillment of a specified requirement. See also **defect**.

nondestructive testing and evaluation (NDT, NDE)—Testing and evaluation methods that do not damage or destroy the product being tested.

normal inspection—Inspection used in accordance with a sampling plan under ordinary circumstances.

100% inspection—Inspection of all the units in the lot or batch.

operating characteristic curve (OC curve)—A graph used to determine the probability of accepting lots as a function of the lots' or processes' quality level when using various sampling plans. There are three types: type A curves, which give the probability of acceptance for an individual lot coming from finite production (will not continue in the future); type B curves, which give the probability of acceptance for lots coming from a continuous process; and type C curves, which (for a continuous sampling plan) give the long-run percentage of product accepted during the sampling phase.

operational qualification (OQ)—Establishing by objective evidence process control limits and action levels that result in product that meets all predetermined requirements.

outlier—An observation point that is distant from other observations. Abnormal responses resulting from special causes or uncontrolled influences that occur during an experiment.

out-of-control process—A process in which the statistical measure being evaluated is not in a state of statistical control. In other words, the variations between the observed sampling results cannot be attributed to a constant system of chance causes.

***p*-chart.** See **percent chart**.

percent chart—A control chart for evaluating the stability of a process in terms of the percentage of the total number of units in a sample in which an event of a given classification occurs. Also referred to as a *proportion chart*.

performance qualification (PQ)—Establishing by objective evidence that the process, under anticipated conditions, consistently produces a product that meets all predetermined requirements.

process average quality—Expected or average value of process quality.

process capability—A statistical measure of the inherent process variability of a given characteristic. The most widely accepted formula for process capability is six sigma.

process capability index—The value of the tolerance specified for the characteristic divided by the process capability. The several types of process capability indexes include the widely used C_{pk} and C_p.

process control—The method for keeping a process within boundaries; the act of minimizing the variation of a process.

process performance qualification (PPQ). See **performance qualification (PQ)**.

process quality—The value of percentage defective or of defects per hundred units in product from a given process. Note: The symbols p and c are commonly used to represent the true process average in fraction defective or defects per unit, and "$100p$" and "$100c$" the true process average in percentage defective or in defects per hundred units.

process validation—Establishing by objective evidence that a process consistently produces a result or product meeting its predetermined requirements.

process validation protocol—A document stating how validation will be conducted, including test parameters, product characteristics, manufacturing equipment, and decision points on what constitutes acceptable test results.

producer's risk—For a given sampling plan, refers to the probability of not accepting (or rejecting) a good lot, Usually, the designated value will be the acceptable quality limit (AQL).

quality—A subjective term for which each person or sector has its own definition. In technical usage, quality can have two meanings: (1) the characteristics of a product or service that bear on its ability to satisfy stated or implied needs, or (2) a product or service free of deficiencies. According to Joseph Juran, quality means "fitness for use"; according to Philip Crosby, it means "conformance to requirements."

quality assurance/quality control (QA/QC)—Two terms that have many interpretations because of the multiple definitions for the words "assurance" and "control." For example, *assurance* can mean the act of giving confidence, the state of being certain, or the act of making certain; *control* can mean an evaluation to indicate needed corrective responses, the act of guiding, or the state of a process in which the variability is attributable to a constant system of chance causes. (For a detailed discussion on the multiple definitions, see ANSI/ISO/ASQ A3534-2 *Statistics—Vocabulary and symbols—Statistical quality control*.) One definition of quality assurance is all the planned and systematic activities implemented within the quality system that can be demonstrated to provide confidence that a product or service will fulfill requirements for quality. One definition for quality control is the operational techniques and activities used to fulfill requirements for quality. Often, however, *quality assurance* and *quality control* are used interchangeably, referring to the actions performed to ensure the quality of a product, service, or process.

random cause—A cause of variation due to chance and not assignable to any factor.

random sampling—A commonly used sampling technique in which sample units are selected so all combinations of n units under consideration have an equal chance of being selected as the sample.

range (statistical)—The measure of dispersion in a data set (the difference between the highest and lowest values).

range chart (R chart)—A control chart in which the subgroup range, R, evaluates the stability of the variability within a process.

reduced inspection—Inspection in accordance with a sampling plan requiring smaller sample sizes than those used in normal inspection. Reduced inspection is used in some inspection systems as an economy measure when the level of submitted quality is sufficiently good and other stated conditions apply. Note: The criteria for determining when quality is "sufficiently good" must be defined in objective terms for any given inspection system.

repeatability—The variation in measurements obtained when one measurement device is used several times by the same person to measure the same characteristic on the same product.

reproducibility—The variation in measurements made by different people using the same measuring device to measure the same characteristic on the same product.

root cause—A factor that caused a nonconformance and should be permanently eliminated through process improvement.

run chart—A chart showing a line connecting numerous data points collected from a process running over time.

sample—In acceptance sampling, one or more units of product (or a quantity of material) drawn from a lot for purposes of inspection in order to reach a decision regarding acceptance of the lot.

sample size (n)—The number of units in a sample.

sample standard deviation chart (s-chart)—A control chart in which the subgroup standard deviation, s, is used to evaluate the stability of the variability within a process.

sampling at random—As commonly used in acceptance sampling theory, the process of selecting sample units so all units under consideration have the same probability of being selected. Note: Equal probabilities are not necessary for random sampling; what is necessary is that the probability of selection be ascertainable. However, the stated properties of published sampling tables are based on the assumption of random sampling with equal probabilities. An acceptable method of random selection with equal probabilities is the use of a table of random numbers in a standard manner.

script—A program or sequence of instructions that is interpreted or carried out by another program rather than by the computer.

sigma—One standard deviation in a normally distributed process.

simulant—Materials used to mimic production product. Typically, rejected parts are used for validation purposes if the cost of actual parts is cost prohibitive.

single sampling—Sampling inspection in which the decision to accept or to reject a lot is based on the inspection of one sample.

Six Sigma—A methodology that provides organizations tools to improve the capability of their business processes. This increase in performance and decrease in process variation leads to defect reduction and improvement in profits, employee morale, and quality of products or services. *Six Sigma quality* is a term generally used to indicate that a process is well controlled (±6σ from the centerline in a control chart).

Six Sigma quality—A term generally used to indicate process capability in terms of process spread measured by standard deviations in a normally distributed process.

software—Instructions that direct a computer to perform specific tasks or operations.

software validation—Confirmation by examination and provision of objective evidence that software specifications conform to user needs and intended uses, and that the particular requirements implemented through software can be consistently fulfilled.

software verification—Provision of objective evidence that the design outputs of a particular phase of the software development life cycle meet all of the specified requirements for that phase.

special causes—Causes of variation that arise because of special circumstances. They are not an inherent part of a process. Special causes are also referred to as *assignable causes*. See also **common causes**.

specification—A document that states the requirements to which a given product or service must conform.

standard—The metric, specification, gage, statement, category, segment, grouping, behavior, event, or physical product sample against which the outputs of a process are compared and declared acceptable or unacceptable.

standard deviation (statistical)—A computed measure of variability indicating the spread of the data set around the mean.

statistical process control (SPC)—The application of statistical techniques to control a process; often used interchangeably with the term *statistical quality control*.

statistical quality control (SQC)—The application of statistical techniques to control quality. Often used interchangeably with the term *statistical process control*, although statistical quality control includes acceptance sampling, which statistical process control does not.

statistics—A field that involves tabulating, depicting, and describing data sets; a formalized body of techniques characteristically involving attempts to infer the properties of a large collection of data from inspection of a sample of the collection.

tightened inspection—Inspection in accordance with a sampling plan that has stricter acceptance criteria than those used in normal inspection. Tightened inspection is used in some inspection systems as a protective measure when the level of submitted quality is sufficiently poor. The higher rate of rejections is expected to lead suppliers to improve the quality of submitted product. Note: The criteria for determining when quality is "sufficiently poor" must be defined in objective terms for any given inspection system.

tolerance—The maximum and minimum limit values a product can have and still meet customer requirements.

trend—The graphical representation of a variable's tendency, over time, to increase, decrease, or remain unchanged.

trend control chart—A control chart in which the deviation of the subgroup average, $\bar{X}$, from an expected trend in the process level is used to evaluate the stability of a process.

type I error—An incorrect decision to reject something (such as a statistical hypothesis or a lot of products) when it is acceptable.

type II error—An incorrect decision to accept something when it is unacceptable.

***u*-chart**—Count-per-unit chart.

unit—An object for which a measurement or observation can be made; commonly used in the sense of a "unit of product," the entity of product inspected to determine whether it is defective or non-defective.

unit sampling—Sequential sampling inspection in which, after each unit is inspected, the decision is made to accept a lot, reject it, or inspect another unit.

upper control limit (UCL)—Control limit for points above the central line in a control chart.

validation—The act of confirming that a product or service meets the requirements for which it was intended.

variables data—Measurement information. Control charts based on variables data include average ($\bar{X}$) chart, range (R) chart, and sample standard deviation (s) chart (see also **range chart**).

variation—A change in data, characteristic, or function caused by one of four factors: special causes, common causes, tampering, or structural variation (see **special causes** and **common causes**).

verification—Confirmation by examination and provision of objective evidence that the specified requirements have been fulfilled.

X and mR chart—Control chart used when working with one sample per subgroup. The moving individual samples are plotted on the $\bar{X}$ chart rather than the subgroup range averages. The individuals chart is always accompanied by a moving range chart, usually using two subgroups to calculate the moving range points.

$\bar{X}$ **chart**—Average chart.

$\bar{X}$ **and** R **chart**—For variables data, control charts for the averages and range of subgroups of data.

Bibliography

Allen, D. 2009. "Validating Test Methods." PMP News. *Packaging Digest.* January 1. Accessed April 26, 2016. http://www.packagingdigest.com/testing/pmp-validating-test-methods-090101.

American Society for Quality (ASQ). Undated. ASQ Quality Glossary. Accessed 5/18/16. asq.org.glossary/.

Code of Federal Regulations. 2014. Title 21, Part 820, *Quality System Regulation.* Washington, D.C.: US Government Printing Office.

Durivage, M. A. 2014. *Practical Engineering, Process, and Reliability Statistics.* Milwaukee: ASQ Quality Press.

———. 2015. *Practical Attribute and Variable Measurement Systems Analysis (MSA): A Guide for Conducting Gage R&R Studies and Test Method Validations.* Milwaukee: ASQ Quality Press.

———. 2016. *Practical Design of Experiments (DOE): A Guide for Optimizing Designs and Processes.* Milwaukee: ASQ Quality Press.

Duvernoy, J., and A. Dubois. 2006. *Instruments and Observing Methods.* Report no. 86. World Metrological Organization. WMO/TD-No. 1306. Beijing.

Eurolab. 1996. EL1545/96 *Validation of Test Methods: General Principles and Concepts.* (December).

European Parliament. Council Directive 93/42/EEC. 1993. Council Directive 93/42/EEC concerning medical devices. Accessed May 5, 2016. http://eur-lex.europa.eu/LexUriServ/LexUriServ.do?uri=CONSLEG:1993L0042:20071011:en:PDF.

FDA. 2002. *General Principles of Software Validation*; *Final Guidance for Industry and FDA Staff.* FDA online. Accessed February 18, 2015. http://www.fda.gov/RegulatoryInformation/Guidances/ucm085281.htm.

———. 2011. *Guidance for Industry: Process Validation: General Principles and Practices.* FDA online. Accessed March 7, 2016. http://www.fda.gov/downloads/Drugs/Guidances/UCM070336.pdf.

———. 2014. "Glossary of Computer System Software Development Terminology (8/95)." FDA online. Accessed 4/28/16. http://www.fda.gov/ICECI/Inspections/InspectionGuides/ucm074875.htm.

———. 2014. "Warning Letter: Oxysure Systems, Inc. 12/8/14." FDA online. Accessed February 21, 2015. http://www.fda.gov/ICECI/EnforcementActions/WarningLetters/ucm429563.htm.

———. 2014. "Warning Letter: Customed, Inc. 12/9/14." FDA online. Accessed February 21, 2015. http://www.fda.gov/ICECI/EnforcementActions/WarningLetters/ucm433090.htm.

———. 2016. "Inspection Observations." FDA online. Accessed April 28, 2016. http://www.fda.gov/ICECI/Inspections/ucm250720.htm.

The Global Harmonization Task Force (GHTF). 2004. SG3 *Quality Management Systems—Process Validation Guidance*. 2nd ed. GHTF.

Gogates, G. 2012. "Software Validation in Accredited Laboratories: A Practical Guide." American Association for Laboratory Accreditation. Accessed 4/27/2016. http://www.a2la.net/guidance/adequate_for_use.pdf.

Government of Canada. 2015. SOR/98-282 *Medical Device Regulations*. Accessed 4/28/16. http://laws-lois.justice.gc.ca/eng/regulations/sor=98=282/.

Hampel, F. R. 1971. "A General Qualitative Definition of Robustness." *Annals of Mathematical Statistics* 42 (6): 1887–96.

———. 1974. "The Influence Curve and Its Role in Robust Estimation." *Journal of the American Statistical Association* 69 (346): 383–93.

Iglewicz, B., and D. C. Hoaglin. 1993. *How to Detect and Handle Outliers*. Milwaukee: ASQ Quality Press.

International Organization for Standardization (ISO). 2004. ISO 13485:2003 *Medical devices—Quality management systems—Requirements for regulatory purposes*. Geneva: ISO.

———. 2005. ISO/IEC 17025:2005 *General requirements for the competence of testing and calibration laboratories*.

———. 2007. ISO 14971:2007 *Medical devices—Application of risk management to medical devices*. Geneva: ISO.

———. 2008. ISO 9001:2008 *Quality management systems—Requirements*. Geneva: ISO.

———. 2012. EN ISO 13485:2012. *Medical devices—Quality management systems—Requirements for regulatory purposes*. Geneva: ISO.

———. 2013. ISO/IEC 26550:2013 *Software and systems engineering—Reference model for product line engineering and management*. Geneva: ISO.

———. 2015. ISO 9001:2015 *Quality management systems—Requirements*. Geneva: ISO.

Lorette, K. Undated. "How Do I Write a Policy Statement for a Business?" *Houston Chronicle* online. Accessed March 12, 2015. http://smallbusiness.chron.com/write-policy-statement-business-3128.html.

Mehta, B. 2013. *Implementing ISO/IEC 17025:2005: A Practical Guide*. Milwaukee: ASQ Quality Press.

Ministry of Health, Labour, and Welfare (Japan). 2004. Ministerial Ordinance No. 169. *Ordinance on Standards for Manufacturing Control and Quality Control for Medical Devices and In-Vitro Diagnostic Reagents*. Tokyo: MHLW. Accessed February 18, 2015. http://www.pmda.go.jp/english/service/pdf/ministerial/050909betsu3.pdf.

National Institutes of Science and Technology (NIST). Undated. "What Is Design of Experiments (DOE)?" NIST online. Accessed March 15, 2015. http://www.itl.nist.gov/div898/handbook/pmd/section3/pmd31.htm.

Payne, G. C. 2005. "Calibration: What Is It?" *Quality Progress* (May). Accessed April 26, 2016. http://asq.org/quality-progress/2005/05/measure-for-measure/calibration-what-is-it.html.

Process Pro. "Ten Steps to Software Validation." 2013. Accessed April 27, 2016. http://www.processproerp.com/wp-content/uploads/10-steps-to-software-validation1.pdf.

Saxton, B. W. 2001. "Reasons, Regulations, and Rules: A Guide to the Validation Master Plan." *Pharmaceutical Engineering*. (May/June).

Sundararajan, K. Undated. "Design of Experiments—A Primer." iSixSigma online. Accessed March 15, 2015. http://www.isixsigma.com/tools-templates/design-of-experiments-doe/design-experiments-%E2%90%93-primer/.

Troutman, R. 2007. "Test Method Validation." Presentation at the 2007 Health Pack Medical Device Packaging Conference.

United Nations Industrial Development Organization (UNIDO). 2006. *Role of Measurement and Calibration in the Manufacture of Products for the Global Market: A Guide for Small and Medium-Sized Enterprises.* Working paper. Vienna: UNIDO.

Walfish, S. 2006. "A Review of Statistical Outlier Methods." *Pharmaceutical Technology* (November).

Wise, S. A., and D. C. Fair. 1998. *Innovative Control Charting.* Milwaukee: ASQ Quality Press.

Index

A

acceptable quality level (AQL), 66
acceptance criteria, failure to define, 112
accuracy, versus precision, 73
ANSI/ASQ Z1.4–2003 (R2013) standard, 66
ANSI/ASQ Z1.9–2003 (R2013) standard, 66
ANSI/ASQC Q3–1988 standard, 66
approvals, in validation documents, failure to obtain, 111
AS9100 standard, 32
attributes data, 65
    process capability for, 104
automated processes, QSR regulations for, 50

B

blocking, in design of experiments, 24

C

calibration
    importance of, 25–26
    QSR regulations for, 6
calibration standards, 26
career development training, 31
c-charts, 81
certification
    versus QSR compliance, under FDA, 11
    requirements, for process validation, 3–12
change control, 111
chi-square, distribution of (Appendix A), 115–16
Code of Federal Regulations
    21 CFR, Part 11, 3, 50
    21 CFR, Part 820, Subpart G, 4–7, 17
        Section 820.3, 13
        Section 820.30, 49–50
        Section 820.70, 4–6, 50
        Section 820.72, 6
        Section 820.75, 3, 6–7, 11, 35–36
commercial off-the-shelf software, validation of, 51
comparative approach, in test method validation, 29
compliance, QSR, versus certification, under FDA, 11
continuous process monitoring, failure to perform, 111
control chart constants (Appendix B), 117
control charts
    for continuous process monitoring, 71–93
    interpretation, 71–73
    rules for, 72–73
    types and selection, 71
controllable input factors, in design of experiments, 24
C_p, 103–4
C_{pk}, 103–4
C_r, 103–4
critical to quality (CtQ) characteristics, 60
custom software, validation of, 51

D

data collection and analysis, statistical methods for, 40
Dean and Dixon outlier test, 97
    critical values of (Appendix C), 119
decision tree, 18
design controls, QSR regulations for, 49
design of experiments (DOE), 23–24, 60
    definition of, 23
design validation, QSR regulations for, 49
deviations
    handling, under process validation procedure, 19–20
    opening, investigation, and closing, 107
Dixon's Q test, 96
dunnage, using for operational qualification, 108

E

electronic records/signatures, QSR regulations for, 50
EN ISO 14971:2012 standard, 17
environmental factors, in test method validation, 28–29
equipment
  operational qualification considerations for, 38
  identical, failure to validate, 110
establish, definition under QSR, 13
Europe, regulatory requirements for process validation, 3–4
European Medical Device Directive (MDD), 11

F

failure mode and effects analysis (FMEA), 60
FDA form 483 observations, process validation in, 1, 7
first article inspection (FAI), 108–9
first article layout (FAL), 108–9
Food and Drug Administration (FDA)
  process validation in form 483 observations, 1
  requirements for software validation, 49–50
  requirements relating to process validation, 4–7
  failure to comply with, 7–9

G

gage repeatability and reproducibility (GR&R) study, 110
Gantt chart, 7
gap analysis, in software validation, 56
Global Harmonization Task Force (GHTF) Study Group 3, 46
group training, 31
Grubbs outlier test, 98–99
  critical values for (Appendix D), 121–22

H

Hampel's method for outlier detection, 100–102
Health Canada, 3
human factors, in test method validation, 28
hypothesis testing, in design of experiments, 24

I

in control process, 71

inspection, measuring, and test equipment (IMTE)
  QSR regulations for, 6
  using uncalibrated, 110
inspection instructions (IIs), 40
installation qualification (IQ), 18–19, 37, 63, 111
instrumental factors, in test method validation, 28
interaction, in design of experiments, 24
ISO (International Organization for Standardization), requirements for process validation, 10
ISO 9001:2008 standard, 17, 32
ISO 11607-1:2009 standard, 29
ISO 13485 standard, 11, 32
ISO 13485:2003 standard, 10, 17
ISO 13485:2012 standard, 10
ISO/IEC 17025:2005 standard, 25, 32

L

limits testing, in operational qualification, 38
line clearance, failure to perform, 107
lot numbers, failure to record, 109
lot-release testing, 40
lots, determining appropriate number for sampling, 69

M

machines, identical, failure to validate, 110
manufacturing process instructions (MPIs), 40
master validation list, 44
master validation plan (MVP), 36, 43–47, 54, 59
  content, 43–44
  failure to document, 111
master validation report (MVR), 40
measurement system, failure to verify, 110
measurement systems analysis (MSA), 110
metrology
  definition under World Meteorological Organization, 25
  importance of, 25–26
MHLW Ministerial Ordinance 169 (Japan), 3
modified off-the-shelf software, validation of, 51

N

National Institute of Standards and Technology (NIST), 26
new employee orientation, in training, 30
93/42/EEC medical device directive, 11
np-charts, 86

O

on-the-job training, 32
operational qualification (OQ), 18–19, 38–39, 63, 111
  disposition of product produced during, 108
  using a simulant or dunnage for, 108
outlier detection
  based on the interquartile range, 95–96
  Dean and Dixon outlier test, 97–98
  Dixon's Q test, 96
  Grubbs outlier test, 98–99
  Hampel's method, 100–102
  Walsh's outlier test, 99–100
outliers, 95–102
out-of-control process, 71–73
output measures, in design of experiments, 24

P

part family, process validation bracketing strategy, 108
p-charts, 88–90
performance qualification (PQ), 18–19, 39, 63, 111
Pharmaceutical Inspection Convention/Pharmaceutical Inspection Co-operation Scheme, 43–44
PI 006-3 PIC/S guidance, 43–44
planning, for process validation, 36
policies and procedures, process validation, establishing, 13–21
  purpose for, 13–14
P_p, 103–4
P_{pk}, 103–4
P_r, 103–4
precision, versus accuracy, 73
process
  in control (stable), 71
  out of control (unstable), 71–73
process capability, 103–5
  for attributes data, 104
  for variables data, 103–4
process failure mode and effects analysis (PFMEA), 36
process monitoring
  after validation, 40
  continuous, failure to perform, 111
  under process validation procedure, 20
process performance qualification (PPQ), 18–19, 39, 63, 111
process scoping, 36–37
process validation
  considerations in, 35–41
  definition under QSR, 13
  FDA form 483 observation findings, 1
    failure to comply with, 7–9
  life cycle, 59–60
  planning, 36
  policies and procedures, establishing, 13
    purpose for, 13–14
  practical, procedures that support, 15–16
  prerequisites, 23–33
  QSR requirements for, 6–7
  repetition of, 40–41
  reporting, 40
  validation versus verification in, 35–36
  verification versus validation in, 35–36
process validation procedure, writing, 16–21
process variation, in test method validation, 27
processes, operational qualification considerations for, 38–39
production and process controls, QSR regulations for, 4–6, 50
project plan, for software development, 54

Q

quality management system (QMS), training, 31
Quality Management Systems—Process Validation Guidance, GHTF Study Group 3, 46
Quality System Regulation (QSR)
  compliance, versus certification, 11
  process validation requirements, 3, 4–7
quality system training, 31

R

RDC 16/2013 standard, 3
regulatory requirements, for process validation, 3–12
reliability estimate
  when sample size is provided, 67
  when sample sizes are specified, 68–69
replication, in design of experiments, 24
responses, in design of experiments, 24
retrospective validation, 59–62
  establishing criteria and intervals for, 109–10
revalidation, 40–41, 59–60, 62–63
  establishing criteria and intervals for, 109–10
  requirements under process validation procedure, 20–21
  of software, 58

S

sample size

considerations, 65–69
failure to justify, 111
sample size calculation, with failures allowed, 67–68
sample size determination, based on confidence and reliability with zero failures allowed, 66–67
samples, failure to produce enough, 109
sampling plan standards, 66
scientific approach, in test method validation, 29
scoping of processes, in process validation, 36–37
self-training, 31
service providers, third-party, in process validation, 32
simulant, using for operational qualification, 108
software development life cycle, 52–53
software validation, 49–58
    completion, 58
    decision tree, 54
    definition of, 50–51
    determining the need for, 50–51
    functional specifications document, 56
    gap analysis, 56
    installation protocol, 56
    installation report, 56
    master validation plan (MVP), 54
    project plan, 54
    revalidation, 58
    system release/go-live, 57
    testing protocols, 57
    validation report, 57
SOR/98-282 standard, 3
Squeglia, Nicholas, 66
stable process, 71
statistical process control (SPC), 26
Sundararajan, K., 23–24

T

test method validation (TMV), 27–29
third-party service providers, in process validation, 32
tool qualification, 110
tooling, identical, failure to validate, 110
traceability matrix, in software development, 53
training, 109
    basic program requirements, 30
    documentation of, 32
    methodology, 31–32
    as prerequisite to process validation, 29–32
training matrix, 30

U

u-charts, 83–85
uncontrollable input factors, in design of experiments, 24
United Nations Industrial Development Organization (UNIDO), 26
unstable process, 71–73
user requirements document, in software development, 54

V

validation
    common issues in, 107–12
    definition under ISO 8402 standard, 27
    definition under QSR, 13
    determining the need for, 45–47
    of software, 49–58
        determining the need for, 50–51
        FDA regulations for, 49–50
    versus verification, 35–36, 45–46
validation master plan (VMP), 36, 43–47, 54, 59
    content, 43–44
    failure to document, 111
validation policy statement, 14
validation report, under process validation procedure, 20
variables data, 65
    process capability for, 103–4
verification, versus validation, 35–36, 45–46

W

Walsh's outlier test, 99–100
Warning Letter, FDA, 7
    examples of, 8–9
worst-case testing, in operational qualification, 38

X

$\bar{X}$ and mR control charts, 91
$\bar{X}$ and R control charts, 73–77
$\bar{X}$ and s control charts, 78

Z

Zero Acceptance Number Sampling Plans (C = 0), 66

The Knowledge Center
www.asq.org/knowledge-center

Learn about quality. Apply it. Share it.

ASQ's online Knowledge Center is the place to:

- Stay on top of the latest in quality with Editor's Picks and Hot Topics.
- Search ASQ's collection of articles, books, tools, training, and more.
- Connect with ASQ staff for personalized help hunting down the knowledge you need, the networking opportunities that will keep your career and organization moving forward, and the publishing opportunities that are the best fit for you.

Use the Knowledge Center Search to quickly sort through hundreds of books, articles, and other software-related publications.

www.asq.org/knowledge-center

TRAINING CERTIFICATION CONFERENCES MEMBERSHIP **PUBLICATIONS**

Ask a Librarian

Did you know?

- The ASQ Quality Information Center contains a wealth of knowledge and information available to ASQ members and non-members

- A librarian is available to answer research requests using ASQ's ever-expanding library of relevant, credible quality resources, including journals, conference proceedings, case studies and Quality Press publications

- ASQ members receive free internal information searches and reduced rates for article purchases

- You can also contact the Quality Information Center to request permission to reuse or reprint ASQ copyrighted material, including journal articles and book excerpts

- For more information or to submit a question, visit
  http://asq.org/knowledge-center/ ask-a-librarian-index

Visit www.asq.org/qic for more information.

TRAINING   CERTIFICATION   CONFERENCES   MEMBERSHIP   **PUBLICATIONS**

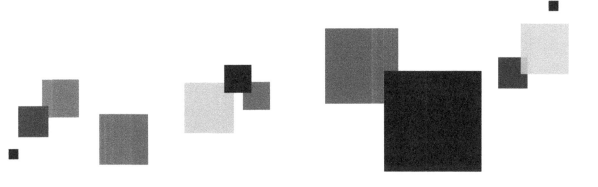

Belong to the Quality Community!

Established in 1946, ASQ is a global community of quality experts in all fields and industries. ASQ is dedicated to the promotion and advancement of quality tools, principles, and practices in the workplace and in the community.

The Society also serves as an advocate for quality. Its members have informed and advised the U.S. Congress, government agencies, state legislatures, and other groups and individuals worldwide on quality-related topics.

Vision

By making quality a global priority, an organizational imperative, and a personal ethic, ASQ becomes the community of choice for everyone who seeks quality technology, concepts, or tools to improve themselves and their world.

ASQ is...

- More than 90,000 individuals and 700 companies in more than 100 countries

- The world's largest organization dedicated to promoting quality

- A community of professionals striving to bring quality to their work and their lives

- The administrator of the Malcolm Baldrige National Quality Award

- A supporter of quality in all sectors including manufacturing, service, healthcare, government, and education

- YOU

Visit www.asq.org for more information.

TRAINING   CERTIFICATION   CONFERENCES   MEMBERSHIP   **PUBLICATIONS**

ASQ Membership

Research shows that people who join associations experience increased job satisfaction, earn more, and are generally happier*. ASQ membership can help you achieve this while providing the tools you need to be successful in your industry and to distinguish yourself from your competition. So why wouldn't you want to be a part of ASQ?

Networking

Have the opportunity to meet, communicate, and collaborate with your peers within the quality community through conferences and local ASQ section meetings, ASQ forums or divisions, ASQ Communities of Quality discussion boards, and more.

Professional Development

Access a wide variety of professional development tools such as books, training, and certifications at a discounted price. Also, ASQ certifications and the ASQ Career Center help enhance your quality knowledge and take your career to the next level.

Solutions

Find answers to all your quality problems, big and small, with ASQ's Knowledge Center, mentoring program, various e-newsletters, *Quality Progress* magazine, and industry-specific products.

Access to Information

Learn classic and current quality principles and theories in ASQ's Quality Information Center (QIC), *ASQ Weekly* e-newsletter, and product offerings.

Advocacy Programs

ASQ helps create a better community, government, and world through initiatives that include social responsibility, Washington advocacy, and Community Good Works.

Visit www.asq.org/membership for more information on ASQ membership.

*2008, The William E. Smith Institute for Association Research

MEMBERSHIP PUBLICATIONS